KNITTING TIPS & TRADE SECRETS

Knitting Tips & Trade Secrets

Clever Solutions for Better Hand Knitting, Machine Knitting and Crocheting

The Taunton Press

Cover photo: Scott Phillips
Editor: Mary Galpin Barnes
Copy/Production Editor: Diane Sinitsky
Layout Artist: Rosalie Vaccaro

Typeface: Goudy
Paper: S. D. Warren, Somerset Matte, 70 lb.
Printer: Quebecor Printing, Kingsport, Tennessee

Taunton
BOOKS & VIDEOS
for fellow enthusiasts

10 9 8 7 6 5 4
Printed in the United States of America

A THREADS Book

THREADS magazine® is a trademark of The Taunton Press, Inc.
registered in the U.S. Patent and Trademark Office.

The Taunton Press, 63 South Main Street, Box 5506,
Newtown, CT 06470-5506
e-mail: tp@taunton.com

Distributed by Publishers Group West

Library of Congress Cataloging-in-Publication Data

Knitting tips & trade secrets : clever solutions for better hand knitting,
      machine knitting, and crocheting.
            p. cm.
         "A Threads book."
         Includes index.
         ISBN 1-56158-156-9
            1. Knitting.   2. Knitting, Machine.   3. Crocheting.
      TT820.K725 1996
      746.43'2—dc20   96-3075
                                                  CIP

CONTENTS

INTRODUCTION

Any technique that can make your hand knitting, machine knitting, or crocheting easier, or the results better, will also increase the pleasure and satisfaction you derive from your craft. In Knitting Tips & Trade Secrets you will find a wealth of information that can do just that.

Here from the pages of Threads magazine, you will learn how to improve on the slip-slip-knit decrease; how to prevent a tangle of yarns when knitting more than one color in a row; how to ensure that your cardigan fronts or sleeves end up the same length; how to make an even join at the end of a round of single or double crochet; how to avoid a multitude of loose yarn ends on machine knitting; and much, much more.

Whether you are a beginning or an experienced knitter or crocheter, whether you knit or crochet occasionally or regularly, you are sure to find within this collection tips that will enhance your projects.

—Mary Galpin Barnes, editor

Chapter 1

Yarn

YARN TWIST

When individual yarns or threads are being spun on a spindle or wheel, and again when two or more strands are being plied together, the wheel can be turned either clockwise or counterclockwise, resulting in Z- or S-twist respectively.

Clockwise twisting produces diagonal twists in the strand that slant from upper right to lower left, just like the center section of the letter Z, as shown in Fig. 1. Counterclockwise twists produce diagonals that run from upper left to lower right, like the center section of the letter S. If you invert the drawing, you'll notice that the direction of the diagonals doesn't change.

The reasons for choosing one twist over another can be functional or aesthetic. To form a multistrand yarn such as a bouclé, the spinning occurs in several steps: The individual strands may be spun in a Z-twist, then two strands combined with a Z-twist, and the third strand added with an S-twist, which binds the three strands together for stability.

FIGURING YARN REQUIREMENTS

If the yarn you have left is four times the width of the knitting, you'll have enough to complete the row without a knot.
—*Bea Stone, Chestnut Hill, MA*

DIVIDING ONE SKEIN EVENLY

If you have only one remaining skein of yarn, how do you tell if there is enough yarn left to knit any pairs of extras (such as sleeve trims) on a sweater? If you divide the one skein into two equal balls, it is easier to tell. To divide the skein, wind a ball from each end without cutting the yarn. Weigh the balls separately, winding and rewinding until they have the same yardage. Now cut them apart.
—*Liz Violante, Marco Island, FL*

SPORT-WEIGHT AND FINGERING YARN

Sport-weight yarn contains from 1200 to 1700 yds. per lb., or 130 to 185 yds. per 50 g ball, and knits to a gauge of about 6 sts/in. on size 4 to 6 needles. Fingering- or baby-weight yarn is thinner and gives a finer gauge (more stitches and rows per inch), with 1700 to 2800 yds. per lb., or 185 to 300 yds. per 50 g ball. Knitting fingering-weight yarn with size 2 to 4 needles gives a gauge of around 7 sts/in., depending on the yarn, the fiber content, and the tension at which it's knit.

FIG. 1

Clockwise action

Counterclockwise action

FIG. 2

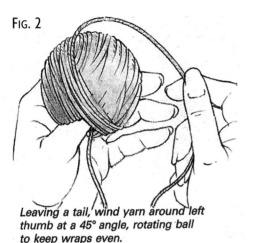

Leaving a tail, wind yarn around left thumb at a 45° angle, rotating ball to keep wraps even.

FIG. 3

WINDING YARN INTO A CENTER-PULL BALL

I prefer to wind my skeined yarn by hand rather than use a mechanical ballwinder, even though it takes longer, because it allows me to become acquainted with the yarn before I knit with it. When the skein is open and untied (you can put it on the back of a chair, on your knees, or in someone else's hands), pinch the tail between your left thumb and forefinger, about a foot from the end. Then, with your left thumb as a pivot, wrap the yarn around it at about a 45° angle (see Fig. 2). Use your left forefinger to move the ball clockwise around your thumb as you wind onto it, keeping the same angle as you wrap the yarn. Be careful not to stretch the yarn, or it will lose its loft. Just guide it from the skein onto your thumb fairly loosely, being careful not to twist it.

If you continue to wind the yarn uniformly like this, you'll finish with a nicely wound ball that's flat on the top and bottom so it will sit in your basket or on the floor without rolling. When you get to the end of the skein, tuck it under several layers of wrapped yarn on the ball. Remove the ball from your thumb and pull the yarn easily from the center, where your thumb used to be.

—Cathy Collier, Edmands, Ashland, OR

MANAGING BALLS OF YARN

After many years of having balls of yarn rolling around and hiding under chairs, I received this simple, but super, tip from a blind friend. Leave about a 5-in. tail when you start wrapping the yarn around your fingers. Wrap as you would any ball, always leaving the tail free. Tuck the other end of the yarn under a strand when you're done. The yarn pulls from the center, and the ball stays put.

—Esther Rumaner, N. Fort Myers, FL

ANOTHER WAY TO WIND A CENTER-PULL BALL

To make a foolproof yarn ball that pulls from the center without tangling, start with a plastic medicine bottle. Place the end of the yarn inside the bottle and snap the cap in place. Wind the yarn loosely around the bottle, keeping the cap above the edge of the ball (see Fig. 3). When all is wound, remove the bottle, release the yarn end, and you have a center-pull ball that won't roll away.

—Lois Carroll, Parma, OH

MAKE SQUISHY YARN BALLS

Winding your yarn too tightly in the ball can make a difference in your knitting or weaving. When the stretched yarn relaxes, the gauge of your piece changes.

To avoid stretching the yarn when you wind a ball, make the first few wraps around your fingers to form the core of the ball. Instead of taking your fingers out of the way of your winding on successive layers, wind the yarn over them. Slip your fingers out and wind the next layer over them. This way you add slack to each layer in the ball and the yarn doesn't stretch.

If you're using a ball- or conewinder and a swift, keep the swift moving a little faster than you're drawing the yarn into the ball or cone. Do this by giving the swift a gentle push to keep some slack in the yarn as it feeds onto the winder. These methods may give you squishy yarn balls, but the yarn will be its own natural size.
—*Carol Hillestad, Cresco, PA*

GREAT YARN HOLDER

Empty baby-wipe containers with flip-up tops make great yarn holders for knitting. Just cut away the center of the lid, place the skein in the container, and pull the yarn up through the hole (see Fig. 4). When you're not knitting, the sealing tab holds the yarn so it doesn't pull out.
—*Darlene McNamara, Willowdale, ON, Canada*

YARN CONTROL

Plastic soda bottles make great yarn caddies for pull-skein yarn. Simply cut a generous hole in the side of a clean soda bottle, slip the skein in and thread the end through the bottle neck. Two-liter bottles will hold a large four-ounce skein, and one-liter bottles work well for one- or two-ounce skeins.
—*Carol Carvalho, Malibu, CA*

HOW TO WIND YARN LOOSELY

When I wind yarn skeins into balls for knitting, I wrap the yarn around four fingers. I slide my fingers out every six wraps to vary the direction of the winding. Then I continue, still winding the yarn around all four fingers and the ball. I get a nice loose ball, and my yarn is never stretched from being wound too tightly.
—*Dorothy Collins, Buffalo, NY*

FIG. 4

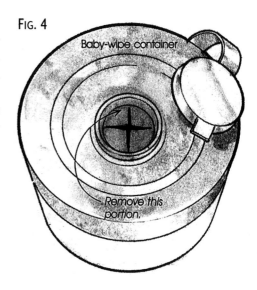

Baby-wipe container

Remove this portion.

FIG. 5

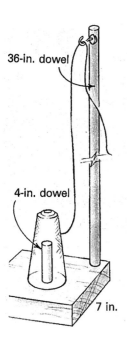

36-in. dowel

4-in. dowel

7 in.

CONE HOLDERS FOR KNITTERS

My husband built me a little stand to help with knitting from cones. He drilled two holes in a 7-in.-sq. block of wood. He set a 4-in. dowel in the center hole to hold the cone and a 36-in. dowel with a cup hook near the top in the corner hole, as shown in Fig. 5. The yarn feeds smoothly into my hands without jerking and pulling.

—*Joan Debolt, Bradford, PA*

KNITTERS NEED BAGGIES!

After winding yarn into a ball on my ball-winder, I slip it into a sandwich bag and fold over the built-in flap. I put the yarn wrapper or some other identification in the bag so I will remember what the yarn is. When I am ready to knit, I punch a hole in the bag and retrieve the center end of the skein. The plastic bag not only keeps the yarn clean but holds the skein together and prevents the yarn from tangling. The yarn flows from the skein smoothly when I am knitting by machine. The uniform, labeled skeins also stack and store nicely.

—*Melissa Yoder, Durham, NC*

TAMING SLIPPERY YARN BALLS

To keep balls of yarn from unraveling while you're knitting, put them in a pouch made from the foot of an old stocking. To make the pouch, cut the foot off midway and make a drawstring by threading waste yarn in and out of the cut edge. Pop the yarn into the pouch, leaving an end hanging out, and pull the drawstring to close the bag. Support hose seem to work especially well.

—*Barbara Eckman, Chicago, IL*

MANAGING RIBBON YARN

When I'm using ribbon yarn, I make a small slit in the lid of a box that fits the ribbon spool and then thread the ribbon through the slit. The spool stays put, and the ribbon won't twist.

—*Avis Irey, Melvern, KS*

COPING WITH ELASTIC THREAD

With all the lovely but inelastic cotton yarns available today, many people are knitting elastic threads into their ribbings along with the yarn. Unfortunately, the spools of elastic can be difficult to manage. I put a large hardbound book on the seat next to me, with the spine against my leg, and lay the spool on its side next to the front edge of the book, with the thread winding off the top of the spool. This setup prevents the spool from rolling around and allows the thread to pay out without tangling.

—*Helen Ettinger, Northbrook, IL*

YARN UNTANGLER

If your knitting yarn becomes tangled and hard to work with, spray it with Static Guard. Static Guard takes the kinks out of the yarn so it will knit or wind smoothly.

—*Doralee Wilson, Libby, MT*

GOOD USE FOR ODD SKEIN

Try knitting your sample swatch from an odd-dye-lot skein, which yarn shops sometimes sell cheaper. I find that this helps me resist the temptation to rip out the sample and reuse the yarn. I can also tell quickly if I really want to purchase the rest of the yarn for a complete project.

—*Louise Owens, Old Hickory, TN*

STORING YOUR YARN COLLECTION

I've never been able to pass up yarn sales. The result: dozens of skeins just waiting for the right project to come along. To keep my yarn in order, as well as dust and moth free, I store it in multilevel hanging sweater bags with clear vinyl fronts. Pop a cedar wood block on every level, and you're set. I use two bags: one for fingering through worsted weight and another for bulky weight.

—*Susan Redlich, Nationa Heights, PA*

KEEPING TABS ON YOUR YARN COLLECTION

I buy lots of yarn wherever I go, and I keep it protected from moths in a huge storage box under a built-in couch. The problem was how to remember what I had without digging through the whole collection. My solution was to take a heavy piece of paper and staple on the yarn label with a yarn sample around it. Next to it I write how many balls I have, where and when it was bought, price, probable use, tension, and needle size. Two of these sheets put my yarn supply at hand at a moment's notice. You could also put the information on index cards.

—*Marion Poller, Herzlyia, Israel*

GOT AN OLD AQUARIUM?

I finally found a good use for an old glass aquarium we had in the garage. I cleaned it thoroughly, hauled it into my knitting area, and then filled it with my leftover yarns. It's convenient, moth-proof, and very pretty!

—*Nadine Skotheim, San Marino, CA*

FIG. 6

VISIBLE YARN STORAGE

Some yarns are too beautiful to be tucked away in a basket or cubbyhole. To get them out where you can enjoy them, hang them on fish stringers—the kind with a chain and snap hooks (see Fig. 6). I hang the stringers from a rafter, up against my studio wall. Each snap hook will take two or three skeins, hung from a tie. And, since they're out in the light and air, insects are less attracted to them.

—*Sharon Lappin Lumsden, Champaign, IL*

MARKING YARN-BALL ENDS

Avid hand knitters tend to acquire lots of yarn balls of odds and ends, which often unravel easily or have hard-to-find ends. To avoid a mess, I secure and mark the yarn ends with a fine metal hairpin tied at the bend with a piece of contrasting yarn. Insert the pin over the tail and into the ball. When you use that yarn again, the end will easily be found!

—*Sue Johnson, Sagle, ID*

MAKE YOUR OWN DESIGNER YARNS

If you have sufficient leftover yarn and thread stashes, you can create new yarns by twisting them together. Combined yarns produce tweedy, colorful textures in sweaters and vests. A favorite sport-weight combination of mine was the result of twining together one strand each of variegated Knit-Cro-Sheen cotton thread, fine fingering wool, baby yarn, and sewing or tatting thread. For a "strawberries and cream" designer yarn, I wind together one strand each of yellow baby yarn; tatting thread in solid white, pink, and yellow; and variegated yellow and pink tatting threads.

If you don't have fine leftover threads or yarns, consider garage sales, secondhand shops, or buying someone else's yarn odds and ends.

—*Sylvia Landman, Novato, CA*

MECHANIZED SWEATER UNWINDING

Unravel a sweater quickly and smoothly by using a hand-held electric mixer. Tie a magazine around one beater. Tape the yarn end to the magazine so it won't slip. While a helper holds the sweater, operate the mixer at low speed, unraveling the yarn and winding it at the same time.

—*Lois Abele, Springfield, VA*

FRESH WOOL FROM RECYCLED SWEATERS

Unraveled yarn from old hand-knitted sweaters comes out looking, and knitting, like brand new wool if you loosely wrap it into skeins, tie each skein in four places, then soak the skeins in warm soapy water, agitating as little as possible. Rinse thoroughly, and hang the skeins to dry before balling. Some of my treasured wools have been knitted into sweaters as many as three times and still look and feel great.
—Helen Benninger, Willowdale, ON, Canada

ANOTHER YARN RECYCLING TIP

After unraveling the yarn from an old sweater or other knitted item you no longer wear, wind it loosely around a cake-cooling rack, then dip the rack into water and let the whole thing dry. All the kinks will be automatically smoothed out, and the yarn will be ready to wind into balls.
—Terry Anderson, Brooksville, FL

STRAIGHTENING CURLY YARN

To recycle used yarn and remove the kinks, run it through this improvised steamer: Take a large coffee can and punch two holes on opposite curved sides, near the top (punch one hole from the outside and one hole from the inside). Fill the coffee can halfway with water and bring the water to a boil directly on the stove. Thread a yarn end through the holes (from the hole punched on the outside to the one punched on the inside, so the yarn doesn't snag), and place a heatproof dish over the top of the can. Mark the end with masking tape so you can find it easily, and slowly pull the yarn through, steaming the entire ball. Let the steamed yarn pile up in a basket. When the yarn has dried, wind into balls and reuse.
—Doralee Wilson, Libby, MT

REJUVENATING LEFTOVER YARN

Leftover or thrift shop yarn is good for small projects such as hats or socks. But many old yarn balls are wound too tightly and need some rejuvenation. To solve this problem with wool yarns, loosely rewind the yarn into a new skein. Hang the yarn on the cardboard portion of a pants hanger in a hot steamy shower, then close the door or curtain tightly and leave it for several hours. The yarn will swell, and once dry will have new life and spring. Severely stressed yarn may have to be plumped more than once.
—Jana Trent, Colleyville, TX

Chapter 2

HAND-KNITTING TECHNIQUES

LONG-TAIL CAST-ON

The long-tail cast-on, also known as the half-hitch cast-on, is probably the most frequently used method for placing knitting stitches on the needle. It's popular because it's easy to execute and results in a neat, elastic edge.

To begin, leave a long end of yarn that's about four times the length of the edge to be cast on, and make a slip knot, as shown in Fig. 7A. Place it on a needle in your right hand with the short end hanging on the side near you.

With the left hand, hold the short end under the last three fingers and make a loop on the left thumb. Insert the needle through the thumb loop, as shown in Fig. 7B. With the right hand, wrap the yarn from the ball around the needle tip from left to right and lift the thumb loop over the needle tip to form a new stitch, as shown in Fig. 7C. Repeat for the required number of stitches.

KEEPING THE FIRST ROUNDS UNTWISTED

When knitting in the round on circular needles, I use hair clips (or spring clothespins for large needles and heavier yarn) to keep the newly cast-on stitches and first few rounds from twisting. Snap one on over the stitches and needle every 15 to 20 stitches. They will slide onto the cable easily and need only a little care when coming back onto the left needle. When the knitting is established, you can take them off.
—*Louise Owens, Old Hickory, TN*

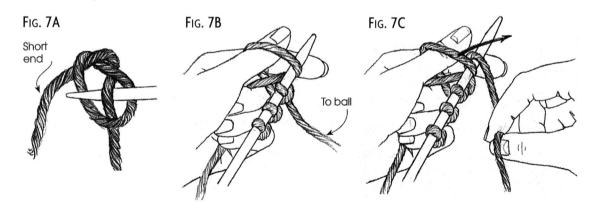

FIG. 7A

Short end

FIG. 7B

To ball

FIG. 7C

STRANDED CAST-ON

Stranded, or open-edge, cast-on results in flexible edges with easily accessed open stitches at the bottom of a piece of knitting. This is especially useful if you want to pick up and work the stitches later, or join the edge to another edge with a joinery cast-off.

To work a stranded cast-on that will be easy to remove later, begin with a main yarn and a length of contrasting yarn. Tie the main and contrasting yarns together at the end, then make a slip knot in the main yarn on a knitting needle, placing the knot on top of the needle. Hold the two strands with the contrasting yarn at bottom, below the thumb.

Cast on by alternating two steps. For step 1, place the tip of the needle behind, then under, the forefinger strand, picking it up to form a loop on the needle (see Fig. 8A). For step 2, place the needle tip under the thumb strand from the front, over and behind the forefinger strand from behind, forming a second loop on the needle as shown in Fig. 8B. Repeat these steps for the required number of stitches.

The stitches will unravel if you release the yarn ends. If you need to pause, make a temporary half hitch after a step-2 stitch by looping a strand of yarn around the needle tip, as shown in Fig. 8C. Be sure to remove the loop before you continue.

After knitting a few rows, you'll notice that the contrasting yarn in the cast-on row simply acts as a stitch holder for the initial stitch loops, as shown in Fig. 8D. To release the open stitches, simply untie the contrasting yarn and remove it.

FIG. 8A

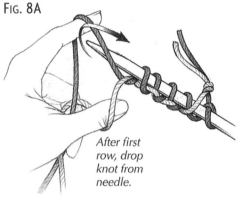

After first row, drop knot from needle.

FIG. 8B

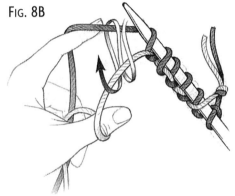

FIG. 8C

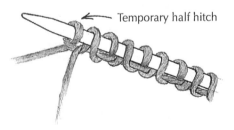

Temporary half hitch

FIG. 8D

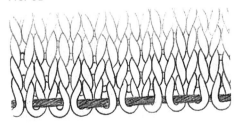

CROCHET PROVISIONAL CAST-ON

For an easy and secure invisible cast-on, you can use the crochet provisional cast-on. Use a smooth, slippery, contrasting yarn for the foundation so it will be easy to find and unravel later. Crochet a chain in the contrast yarn that is one stitch longer than the number of stitches required. Fasten off. With the knitting yarn, pick up a stitch in the back loop of each chain except the last one made, as shown in Fig. 9. This is the first knit row. When you're ready to pick up the loops and knit in the opposite direction, pull the contrast yarn end back through the last chain stitch and unravel the chain.

FIG. 9

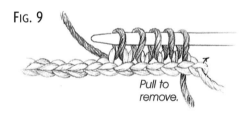

Pull to remove.

KNITTING THE FIRST ROW

When you knit into the first row of simple loop cast-on, also called single cast-on, the extra yarn between the stitches increases in length the farther you knit. To prevent this, open up each stitch as you knit it. Place the right needle into the cast-on loop, and gently pull the needles apart. Then complete knitting the stitch. Keep the needles close together at this stage, and don't pull on the work. Repeating these two steps will keep the stitches open and properly spaced with no extra thread at the end.

—Jean Lucas, Brookfield, CT

EVEN JOINS IN CIRCULAR KNITTING

Here are two techniques for making perfectly smooth rounds of circular knitting with no perceptible joins.

On the cast-on edge, turn and knit back (as for straight knitting) the first row, and *then* join, making certain the edges aren't twisted. This will eliminate the "dog leg," or uneven join, and reverse the cast-on edge to the more attractive, unstranded side (with the garter-stitch bumps). Be sure to establish ribbing or other pattern in straight knit in the first row, and then join for circular knitting.

When you cast off in the round, you can eliminate the uneven join by inserting the needle into the first cast-off stitch, making a stitch, and then casting it off as the final cast-off stitch. This technique pulls the first portion up to make it even with the last stitch, but the double stitch is not noticeable.

—Barbara Rottman, Urbana, OH

KNIT CABLE CAST-ON

For a firm edge that doesn't stretch, begin with knit cable cast-on. You need two stitches on the needle to begin, so make one by placing a slip knot on the left-hand needle; make the second by knitting into the first and transferring the new stitch to the left needle. For subsequent stitches, insert the right needle tip between the first two stitches on the left needle, as shown in Fig. 10. Draw through a loop and transfer it to the left needle. Repeat for the required number of stitches.

FIG. 10

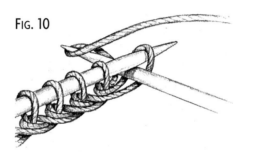

AVOIDING THE DOG LEG IN CIRCULAR KNITTING

My solution to the circular-knitting dog-leg problem is to cast on by using a double technique with one needle and two ends of yarn. At the join, I pick up the "tail," and holding it together with the working yarn, I draw the last and first cast-on stitches closely together. I work the first four stitches with both yarns, then drop the "tail" and work on. Since there's no knot with a double cast-on, the stitches will slide together, and you'll have to use a marker to find the beginning of the round.

—*Shelagh Smith, Brandon, VT*

TUBULAR CAST-ON FOR CIRCULAR KNITTING

I find it helpful when using a tubular cast-on for circular knitting to start as if on straight needles, with an odd number of stitches. When I've finished the tubular rows, I connect the rib into a circle by working the two end stitches together. You can work in the short tail of yarn by using it to join the gap that results when you switch from flat to circular knitting. With these few rows of work and the contrast yarn, you will be much less likely to twist the stitches in joining them.

—*Betty Klahn, Klamath Falls, OR*

NO STAIRSTEPS WHEN CASTING ON

Here's a neat way to avoid knitting stairsteps when casting on at the beginning or end of a row, such as you might need to do for the seams of dolman sleeves. Work to the last stitch of the row and slip it to the right-hand needle, then turn the work. Using the cable cast-off method (shown in Fig. 11), insert the right-hand needle between the first two stitches either knitwise or purlwise as the side of the work dictates. Cast on the required number of stitches, and repeat for as many rows as you need.

—Diane Zangl, Lomira, WI

FIG. 11

At beginning of row, slip needle from front to back between first two stitches, draw through a new stitch, and place stitch on left needle. Repeat for needed stitches.

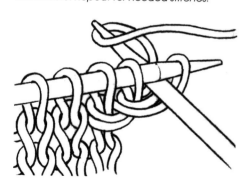

CLEVER CAST-ON AT THE END OF A ROW

When you want to extend the number of stitches at the end of a row, insert a crochet hook in the edge stitch of the second row below your last stitch (see Fig. 12A) and draw up a loop. Make a loose chain of the number of stitches to be cast on (Fig. 12B), then remove the hook and insert the free knitting needle into the loop to make one stitch. Pick up and knit or purl a loop in each remaining chain, bringing the needle up to the last stitch of the completed row, then continue to knit or purl across (Fig. 12C).

—Janet M. Jillson, Grand Forks, ND

GETTING STARTED WITH KNITTING IN THE ROUND

In case you've never tried knitting in the round on a circular needle, here are some tips to get you started: You'll need to join the cast-on row without twisting. After casting on, carefully align all stitches so that they lie in the same direction. To join, hold the end of the needle with the knitting strand in your right hand, slip a marker onto this needle to indicate the beginning of the round, then knit the first stitch from the left-hand needle.

If you knit a sleeve from the cuff to the shoulder in the round, the number of cast-on stitches

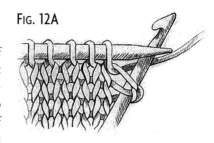

FIG. 12A

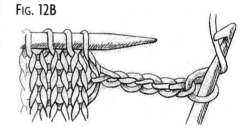

FIG. 12B

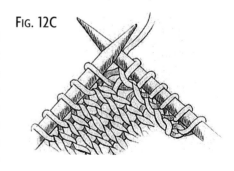

FIG. 12C

may be too few to fit on a circular needle. In this case, divide the stitches between three or four double-pointed needles. First cast on all stitches onto a long needle, then slip them, evenly divided, onto double-pointed needles, taking care not to twist the cast-on row. After several rows with increases have been worked, you can transfer the stitches to a short circular needle.

CASTING ON MID-ROW

To cast on stitches in the middle of a row (for example, when you're replacing the stitches you bound off for a buttonhole) use this version of cable cast-on. Knit to the opening, then *insert the left-hand needle (LHN) between the last two stitches on the right-hand needle (RHN). Wrap the yarn over the LHN (see Fig. 13), and pull a stitch through. Slip this new stitch onto the RHN purlwise.* Repeat *-* for the desired number of stitches, but slip the final stitch onto the RHN knitwise. Complete the row.

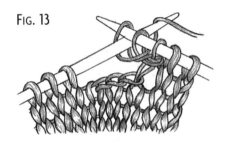

FIG. 13

SINGLE CAST-ON

When you want to make an opening in knitting, such as for buttonholes or the thumb opening in mittens, bind off or hold the required number of stitches. On the next row, use single cast-on to add back the same number of stitches above the gap. When knitting in the round, make the required number of snug loops, as shown in Fig. 14. The ball end of the yarn should come out behind the loop so the stitches will be firm and untwisted.

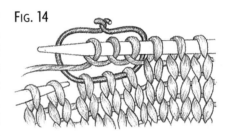

FIG. 14

TO CAST OFF LOOSELY

Whenever a knitting pattern says "cast off loosely," I switch to a needle three sizes larger than the size I've been using for the pattern. I find this much easier than changing my tension, and the results are perfectly even.
—*Jennifer Lobb, Lynden, ON, Canada*

SLIPPED STITCH BIND-OFF

To prevent an enlarged loop at the end of a bound-off row: On the last row before the bind-off row, slip the first stitch as if to purl, then work to the end of the row. Turn and bind off.

—*Leslie Calaway, Roseville, CA*

CASTING OFF

The most popular method for binding or casting off knit and purl stitches is to chain the stitches off the right-hand needle one at a time. You accomplish this by first working two stitches, either knitting or purling to match the stitches in the row below. Then insert the left-hand needle from left to right into the right stitch on the right-hand needle, lift this stitch over the left stitch, and drop the right stitch off the needle. Knit or purl another stitch from the left-hand needle, and repeat the process with the two loops on the right-hand needle, as shown in Fig. 15. Repeat across the row. When there is one stitch remaining, cut the yarn, leaving the end long if it's necessary for sewing, and pull the end through the remaining stitch.

A QUICK BIND-OFF

Binding off a piece of knitting can be difficult if the yarn is heavy or irregular or if the garment is bulky. You can save a lot of time and avoid frustration if you substitute a crochet hook approximately the same diameter as the knitting needle. Put the hook through the first loop on the left-hand needle and knit the stitch onto the hook. Knit the next stitch onto the hook, and pull the new stitch through the first one, as shown in Fig. 16. Continue in this manner to the end of the row, and pull the yarn through the last loop on the hook. This takes me about a tenth of the time of a two-needle bind-off and makes a tight, even edge.

—*Lanette Scapillato, Issaquah, WA*

FIG. 15

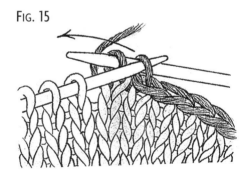

FIG. 16

Knit onto a crochet hook to bind off.

Pull yarn through stitch.

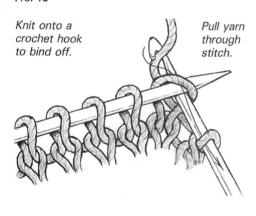

FIG. 17A

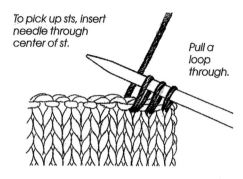

To pick up sts, insert needle through center of st.

Pull a loop through.

FIG. 17B

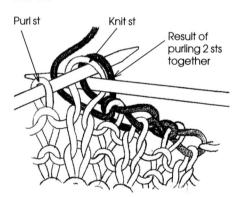

Purl st

Knit st

Result of purling 2 sts together

ADDING RIBBING

To add ribbing to a garment that has already been knitted, you can either pick up stitches along the lower edge of the garment (as shown in Fig. 17A), then knit the ribbing down and cast off, or you can knit the ribbing separately, cast off, and sew it onto the garment. Either way, you'll need a stretchy cast-off edge, as is produced by the following technique, which is good on a knit one, purl one rib: Knit two sts together when the second stitch on the left-hand needle is a knit stitch, as shown in Fig. 17B, and purl two together when the second stitch on the left-hand needle is a purl stitch. Slip the resulting stitch back to the left-hand needle without twisting, and reposition the right needle behind the yarn to prepare for a purl stitch or in front of the yarn to prepare for a knit stitch. Keeping in the rib pattern, repeat this process until all the stitches are cast off.

STRANDED CAST-OFF

The stranded cast-off is the simplest method of securing stitches. It performs the same function as the stranded cast-on (see p. 12). You can also use it to temporarily hold stitches that will be picked up and worked later.

Cut the yarn end about a foot longer than the width of the knitting and thread a blunt tapestry needle. Beginning at the side that has the yarn end, slip the tapestry needle through several stitches on the knitting needle, as shown in Fig. 18; pull the yarn through; and drop the stitches off the knitting needle. Repeat across the row.

FIG. 18

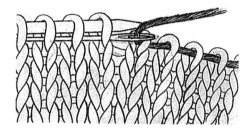

ANOTHER DECORATIVE RIBBING BIND-OFF

When I was completing a gansey that had employed a doubled yarn cast-on and double rib (k2, p2), I wanted to finish the neck and sleeves with an attractive doubled yarn bind-off that complemented the sweater's elaborate knit/purl patterns. The technique I developed produces a pretty braided edge that's very resistant to fraying. On the right side it looks like a braid of twined loops; underneath it has a firm, flat chain of knit V's.

At the beginning of the bind-off row, measure out a sufficiently long strand of yarn to knit together with the strand you're already using. Leave a tail in the new strand to weave into the wrong side, and purl the first 2 sts with both strands held together as one. Pass the first stitch over the second. Continue purling one and passing the previous stitch over to the end of the round, and join the two ends to the first stitch. Then weave all three tails in on the wrong side. If you're knitting flat pieces, be sure to work this bind-off on the right side.

—*Alice DeCamp, Westport, CT*

Avoid going twice into the first two stitches

It's best not to get into the habit of going twice into the first two stitches. First, it isn't strictly necessary. Second, the tubular cast-off is often used to finish necklines worked in rounds. In this case, the last two stitches become the right-hand neighbors of the first two stitches. If you've gone only into the first two stitches, you can go into them a second time at the end of the casting-off sequence and link them to the last two stitches. This gives a totally undetectable join. If you have already gone twice into the first two stitches, you'll have a problem, unless, of course, you started to cast off by linking the first two stitches directly with the last two.

—*Montse Stanley, Cambridge, England*

Tubular cast-off for single rib

Montse Stanley's article, "Knitting a Perfect Rib" (*Threads*, No. 15, p. 46), evoked a lot of response from our readers—new ideas, as well as corrections. We thank Montse Stanley and Betty J. Louie of Carmichael, CA, for pointing out errors in the drawings on tubular cast-off for single and double rib. The corrected drawings are shown in Fig. 19.

FIG. 19A

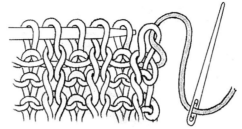

Insert needle knitwise into first (knit) stitch, and drop it. The first time around you go into this stitch only once.

FIG. 19B

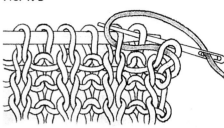

Insert needle purlwise into third (knit) stitch, then purlwise into second (purl) stitch. Drop second stitch. The first time around, you go into it only once.

FIG. 19C

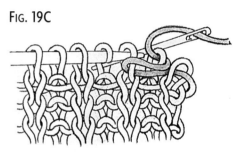

Insert needle knitwise into fourth (purl) stitch, from back. Repeat from beginning.

ALTERNATIVE TUBULAR CAST-OFF FOR SINGLE RIB

Once you learn this beautiful, stretchy cast-off that perfectly matches its cast-on counterpart, it will probably become your favorite. I call it the invisible bind-off. There are a few tricks in the way you think about the process that will make it easy. First, the yarn on the tapestry needle should always go *under* the knitting needle. Second, think about grafting the rib stitches as pairs: a pair of knits, then a pair of purls.

Work two rows of tubular stocking stitch to begin the bind-off: For work beginning and ending with a knit stitch, k1; then sl1 purlwise with the yarn in front. Alternate these two stitches to the end of the row. On the second row, sl1 purlwise with the yarn in front; then put the yarn to the back and k1; repeat these two steps to the end of the row.

If your first stitch is a knit, the knits will be on the front layer, and the purls will be on the back. Starting the bind-off is a little tricky, but once you've entered the first two stitches the first time, from then on you can work in pairs, and a pleasant rhythm develops. Break off a length of yarn about four times as long as the edge you're binding off, and thread a blunt tapestry needle on the end. Hold the work with the right side facing you.

Step 1. The beginning stitches: Insert the tapestry needle into the first knit stitch, as if to

FIG. 20A

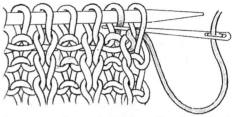

Insert needle purlwise into first knit stitch and knitwise from behind into first purl stitch. Leave both stitches on needle.

purl. Pull the yarn through, and leave the stitch on the knitting needle. Working around from the back, bring the needle to the front between the knit stitch and the next purl stitch, and insert it into the first purl stitch, as if to knit; it's tricky, and it looks as if you're twisting the front leg of the stitch when the needle exits toward the left (see Fig. 20A). Pull the yarn through, leaving the stitch on the knitting needle. Both of the stitches are still on the needle.

Step 2. Work the pairs of knit stitches as follows, remembering that a stitch isn't dropped until the tapestry needle has passed through it twice: Insert the needle knitwise back into the first knit stitch, and drop it. Don't pull the yarn through yet. Insert the needle purlwise into the next knit stitch (third stitch). Leave it on the knitting needle, and pull the yarn through (see

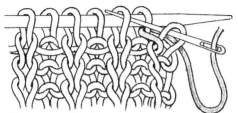

For a pair of knit stitches, insert needle knitwise into first knit stitch, and drop it. Then go purlwise into second knit stitch.

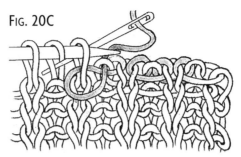

Go purlwise into first purl stitch, and drop it. Loop yarn to right and under knitting needle, and insert tapestry needle knitwise from back into second purl stitch.

Fig. 20B). This completes the work for a pair of knit stitches. Only the first stitch of the pair has been dropped; the second stitch will become the first stitch of the next knit pair.

Step 3. Each pair of purl stitches is worked as follows: Slip the first purl stitch off onto the tapestry needle, as if to purl, but don't pull the yarn through. Loop the yarn to the right and under the knitting needle toward the back. Then insert the needle from the back into the next purl stitch knitwise, as described above. Both of these steps are shown in Fig. 20C. Pull the yarn through, being careful not to pull it too tightly.

Continue grafting pairs of knits and pairs of purls in this manner until you reach the end of the row. Notice that you always insert the tapestry needle into the first stitch of the pair the way you would knit that type of stitch—knitwise into the first knit, purlwise into the first purl—and that this stitch is always dropped. The second stitch of the pair is worked in the opposite manner, and the tapestry needle is always passed out and away from the work.

If the first stitch of the rib is a purl, reverse the order of the tubular rows and the stitches in step 1. Then start working at step 3.
—*Betty J. Louie, Carmichael, CA*

TUBULAR CAST-OFF FOR DOUBLE RIB

The process of casting off a tubular double rib is similar to the process of casting off a tubular single rib, although there are nearly twice as many steps. This time, however, Montse Stanley goes into the first two stitches twice. She says that because the process is so complex, go-ing once into the first stitches would make it even more daunting; besides, the complexity of the structure makes it possible for you to get a good join in circular knitting, even if you have gone into the edge stitches twice.

Work two tubular rows to begin: Knit the first knit stitch of each rib, and slip the second purlwise with yarn in back; purl the first purl stitch,

FIG. 21

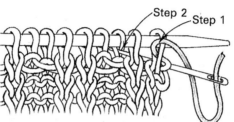

Insert needle purlwise into first knit stitch (step 1). Then, working from back and under knitting needle, insert needle knitwise into first purl stitch (step 2).

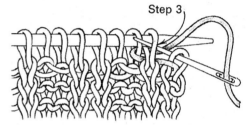

Insert needle knitwise into first knit stitch, looping yarn over top of stitch, and drop it. Then insert needle purlwise into second knit stitch (step 3).

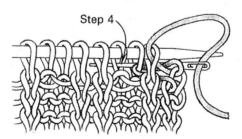

Loop yarn up, and working in back from right to left, insert needle purlwise into first purl stitch, then knitwise into second purl stitch (step 4).

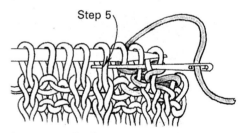

Insert needle knitwise into second knit stitch, and drop it. Insert needle purlwise into third knit stitch (step 5), and drop first purl stitch.

and slip the second purlwise with yarn in front. Two things are crucial for a successful tubular double-rib bind-off: Work around the back knitwise into the purl stitches, just the way you did for the single rib. Also, to avoid twisting the tops of the stitches, be very careful to loop the yarn and insert the needle as shown. Fig. 21 shows a ribbing that begins with two knit stitches.

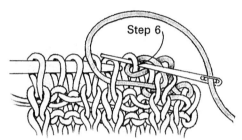

Insert needle purlwise into second purl stitch, and drop it (step 6).

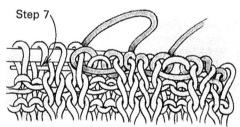

Working around from back, insert needle knitwise into third purl stitch (step 7). Repeat from step 3.

ANOTHER TECHNIQUE FOR TUBULAR CAST-OFF, DOUBLE RIB

I've found an easy way to work tubular cast-off for 2x2 rib. First I transfer the purl stitches onto a double-pointed needle and hold it behind and parallel to the needle with the knit stitches. For work beginning with k2, I treat the first knit stitch as a purl stitch and slip it onto the back needle, as shown in Fig. 22.

I bind off with the same steps I would use for tubular cast-off, single rib (see pp. 20-21, "Alternative tubular cast-off for single rib" drawings). I begin by inserting from the back into the first stitch on the back needle (knit treated as purl) as if to knit. Then I go into the first stitch on the front needle (second knit) as if to purl. These 2 sts remain on their needles, and I work a pair of purls: Slip the first purl off purlwise (the first time this stitch is the knit treated as a purl); then go into the second purl from the back knitwise. Then I work a pair of knits: Slip the first knit off knitwise; then go purlwise into the second knit. Continue in this rhythm—a pair of purls from the back needle, then a pair of knits from the front needle—to the end of the row.

—*Betty J. Louie, Carmichael, CA*

FIG. 22

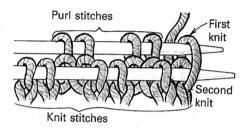

Purl stitches
First knit
Second knit
Knit stitches

Transfer purl stitches to double-pointed needle held behind knit stitches. Treat first knit as a purl to begin tubular bind-off for double rib.

ONE ROW FLAT-CHAIN CAST-OFF

You might want to try my method for a one row flat-chain cast-off as an alternative to Montse Stanley's decrease cast-off. I feel that the smoother edge of this version is more desirable than Stanley's crochetlike finish. On single rib, beginning with a knit stitch, *p2tog and leave the stitch on the right-hand needle. Carry the yarn to the back, k1, and pass the first stitch on the right-hand needle over it. Bring the yarn forward, transfer the stitch from the right-hand needle back to the left-hand needle, and repeat from * to the end of the row.

Work the one row flat-chain cast-off for double rib as follows for work beginning k2: K2, pass the first knit stitch over the second knit stitch. [Bring the yarn forward. *Transfer the stitch from the right-hand needle to the left-hand needle. P2tog. Repeat from * once. Carry the yarn back. **K1, pass the first stitch on the right-hand needle over. Repeat from ** once.] Repeat between [ ] to the end of the row.

—Betty J. Louie, Carmichael, CA

INCREASES AND DECREASES

Decreases and increases in knits can slant either to the left or to the right, adding decorative detail to the knitted fabric. When knitting pairs of increases for a dart, for example, you might balance the dart by working one right-slanting and one left-slanting increase together, or you could slant all the increases toward the outside of the garment. There are many different increases and decreases to choose from, including the following, shown in Fig. 23.

Right-slanting decrease—Knit two together

FIG. 23

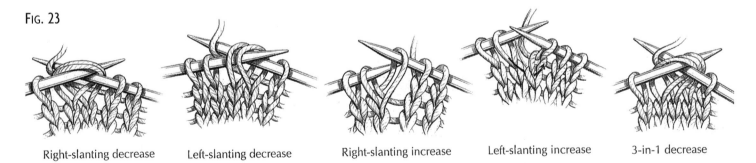

Right-slanting decrease   Left-slanting decrease   Right-slanting increase   Left-slanting increase   3-in-1 decrease

by inserting the right needle into the next two stitches on the left needle and knitting as one.

Left-slanting decrease—Called slip, slip, knit, this decrease is worked by first slipping two stitches knitwise, one at a time, to the right needle; insert the left needle tip from left to right into the front of the slipped stitches; then knit them off together.

Right-slanting increase—Lift the purl loop below the next stitch and place it on the left needle; knit the loop as a normal stitch, then knit the next stitch.

Left-slanting increase—Work this increase like the right-slanting increase, except after the stitch: Knit the stitch, then lift the purl loop two rows below the stitch; untwist the loop, then knit it as a normal stitch.

3-in-1 decrease—Knit three together by inserting the right needle into all three stitches on the left needle and knitting as one.

3-in-1 increase—Work a right-slanting increase, knit the stitch, then work a left-slanting increase on the other side.

Make one

To make 1 stitch (a type of increase) on the purl or knit side, lift the running thread between the stitches on the right and left needles onto the point of the LHN by inserting the LHN from front to back. Knit or purl the new stitch in the back as shown in Fig. 24; it will be twisted. Working the make 1 stitch twisted prevents a hole from forming below it.

Two common decreases

There are several ways to decrease stitches in knitting, and among the most common are slip, slip, knit (ssk) and purl two together (p2tog). Worked on the knit side of the fabric, the ssk decrease slants to the left: Slip two stitches, one at a time, as if to knit. Insert the left needle into these stitches from left to right, as shown in Fig. 25A, and knit them together.

Worked on the purl side of the fabric, the p2tog decrease slants to the right on the knit face of the fabric. To p2tog, insert the right needle into two adjacent stitches and purl them together (see Fig. 25B).

Fig. 24

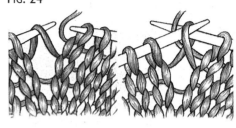

Slip, slip, knit (ssk).

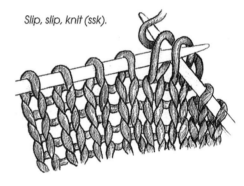

Purl 2 together (p2tog).

FIG. 26

K2tog

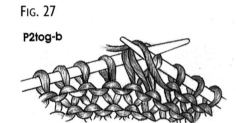

FIG. 27

P2tog-b

KNIT-TWO-TOGETHER DECREASE

The usual way to decrease in knitting is to k2tog (knit two stitches together). This decrease slants toward the right. Insert the right-hand needle knitwise through 2 sts at once as shown in Fig. 26 and knit them together as if they were one stitch.

PURL TWO TOGETHER-BACK

A p2tog-b decrease (purl 2 sts together in the back loops) is the purl-side equivalent of an ssk. This decrease slants toward the left on the purl side. Turn the work over slightly, and insert the tip of the RHN into the backs of the next 2 p sts on the LHN, second stitch first; then wrap the yarn and purl them as one stitch (see Fig. 27).

IMPROVING THE SSK

A favorite knitting technique of mine for decreases that slant to the left is the ssk (slip, slip, knit together), but instead of slipping the 2 sts as if to knit, I slip the first stitch as if to knit and the second as if to purl. Then I insert the left-hand needle to the front of both slipped stitches and knit them together as usual. The slipped purlwise stitch somehow tucks itself very neatly behind the slipped knitwise stitch and

becomes invisible, resulting in a very smooth decrease that slants to the left. Use this method whenever the directions say, sl1-k1-psso, and you'll get a much neater edge.

—*E. Dee Barrington, Ponca City, OK*

LEFT-SLANTING DECREASE

Sl1-k1-psso (slip 1-knit 1-pass slipped st over) is a single decrease that slants toward the left. Slip the first stitch as if to knit. Knit the next stitch. Insert the tip of the left needle into the slipped stitch, as shown in Fig. 28, and pull it over the knitted st.

FIG. 28

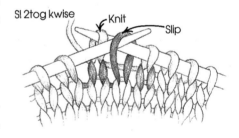

Sl 2tog kwise — Knit — Slip

VERTICAL DOUBLE DECREASE

Sl2tog kwise-k1-p2sso (slip 2 tog-knit 1-pass 2 slipped sts over) is a vertical double decrease. The two side stitches slant inward behind the prominent center st. Slip two stitches as if knitting them together, knit the next st, and pass the two slipped stitches together over the knit st, as shown in Fig. 29.

FIG. 29

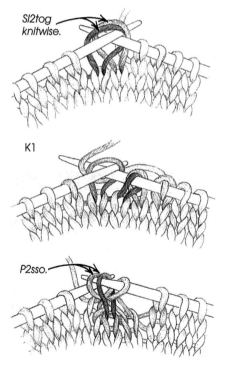

Sl2tog knitwise.

K1

P2sso.

LIFTED INCREASE

The lifted increase adds a stitch almost invisibly. When you get to the point of the increase, insert the right-hand needle (RHN) into the top of the next st in the row below; knit as shown in Fig. 30. Knit the next st on the LHN.

PERFECTLY MATCHED DECREASES

As every knitter knows, when you're working a series of decreases every other row, none of the left-slanting decreases (sl1, k1, psso; k2tog through back loop; or ssk) will produce a truly straight decrease line exactly matching the line of the right-slanting k2tog ones. Now try this: For your right-slanting decreases, k2tog every other knit row as usual, but for your left-slanting decreases, work slip-slip-purls (ssp) on the purl side. To ssp, slip the first two stitches one at a time knitwise (just as you would an ssk)—this twists each stitch. Now replace both stitches, still twisted, onto the left needle and purl them together through the back loops. You'll find that your decrease lines will match perfectly, and both will look as straight as if they had been drawn with a ruler.

—*Janet E. Price, Chicago, IL*

FIG. 30

With tip of LHN, pull st over new st.

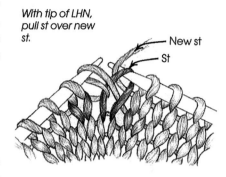

— New st

— St

FIG. 31

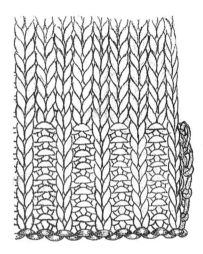

DOUBLE-LAYER RIB

A double-layer rib gives firmness and body to ribbed edges, which can be more compatible with the weight of a heavy garment than a single-layer rib. In ribbing, knit the width of the band normally. To create a fold line, purl a right-side row or knit a wrong-side row, then resume the ribbing stitch and knit the same number of rows again for the second layer, as shown in Fig. 31. With this technique, you can sandwich the raw edge of a garment's lining between the layers of ribbing, then sew the ribbing and lining in place with one row of overcast stitching.

NO-PURL CORRUGATED RIB

Purling the multicolor stripes of Fair Isle corrugated rib gives an unappealing echo of the previous color in the new one. Changing the colors on the knit stripes solves that problem, but since you're stranding two yarns, the rib isn't stretchy like normal k2, p2.

I take advantage of this "drawback." First, I knit all the stitches (no purling), so the color always changes cleanly. Then, I pull the stranded yarn tight in back so the rib puckers like corrugated paper. I'm careful to calculate enough stitches to go over the head and hands and around the hips. I alternate knitting 2 sts in a main color and shading the next 2 sts over the length of the rib from darkest to lightest and back to darkest with yarn from a contrasting color family. To prevent the edge from curling, I pick up the cast-on and add a knit facing later, stitching it inside loosely.

—Alice DeCamp, Westport, CT

STRETCHY KNIT RIBBING

Here's a delicate ribbing called plissé that is very stretchy and yet hugs the waistline beautifully. Use the same needle size as you would to knit any ribbing, and cast on your stitches in multiples of three. Work each row k2, p1 as deep as desired (see Fig. 32).

—Clara Wendrich, Tampa, FL

FIG. 32

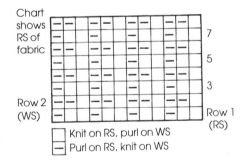

SLIPPING A STITCH

Slip 1 stitch purlwise (sl1 pwise) is a way to move a stitch to the right-hand needle (RHN) without knitting it. Slipping the stitch purlwise also ensures that it will not be twisted when you encounter it on the next row. On RS rows, with yarn in back, insert RHN as if to purl, slipping st in this position onto needle (see Fig. 33). On WS rows, do the same, except with yarn in front.

FIG. 33

Sl 1 pwise

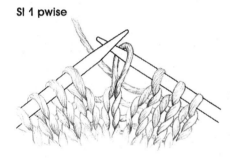

ELONGATED STITCHES

Knit, wrapping yarn around needle twice is a way to make one stitch twice as tall as the others. Insert RHN into stitch as if to knit, then bring yarn over top of needle to back, under needle to front, then over top again before knitting the stitch (see Fig. 34). On the return row, drop one of the loops and work the other as directed, knitting, purling, or slipping it.

FIG. 34

K wrapping yarn twice

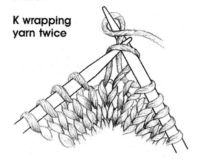

Another useful technique to produce elongated stitches is to knit into the row below. Insert the RHN knitwise into the stitch below the one on the LHN (see Fig. 35). Knit and drop the top stitch, which will be caught in the stitch you've just knit.

FIG. 35

Knit into row below.

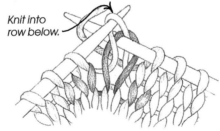

FIG. 36

BC4

FIG. 37

FC4

This bc4 (back cross cable over 4 sts) looks different from a standard back cross cable because it is worked with elongated, slipped stitches. In a back cross cable, *you move stitches from the left to the right on the front of the work.* Slip 2 stitches purlwise to cable needle (cn) and *hold them behind the work;* knit the next 2 stitches; then knit the 2 stitches from cn, wrapping yarn twice for each st (see Fig. 36). The effect is that you have traded position between 2 purl stitches and 2 elongated knit stitches. The purls become elongated knits, and the elongated knits will become purls on the next row.

This fc4 (front cross cable over 4 sts) looks different from a standard front cross cable because it is worked with elongated slipped stitches. The process is the same as bc4 except that you're moving stitches toward the left by holding them in front of the work, and the elongated sts are *not* knit from the cable needle. In a front cross cable, *you move stitches from the right to the left on the front of the work.* Slip the next 2 stitches purlwise to cn and *hold them in front of the work;* knit the next 2 sts wrapping yarn twice for each st; then knit the 2 stitches from cn (see Fig. 37).

TOOL-LESS TWISTS

For twist stitches, you don't need a cable needle, cable hook, or any other tool. For a left twist, slip the two stitches one at a time as if to knit, then put the needle through both and slip them back, as shown in the top drawing of Fig. 38. To make a right twist, slip both stitches as if to knit two together, then slip them back one at a time, as shown in the bottom drawing of Fig. 38. All slips should be made knitwise so that the twists untwist and you end up with the stitches front side to the front.

—Joy Beeson, Voorheesville, NY

FIG. 38

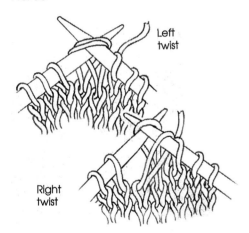

Left twist

Right twist

CAST-ON BOBBLE

Using a cable cast-on to add stitches at any point in a garment between the first two stitches on the left-hand needle is good for making a cast-on bobble. Insert the right-hand needle tip between the next two stitches on the left-hand needle, as shown in Fig. 39. Draw through a loop and transfer it to the left-hand needle. Repeat for the required number of stitches.

HAND KNITTING AS EVEN AS MACHINE KNITTING

I've found that European knitters often use a size smaller needle on the purl side of stockinette stitch than on the knit side. The overall effect is as even as machine knitting with no unsightly spaces between every other row. There's hardly any effect on gauge. One or two extra rows are all I ever need to compensate.

—Billie Gooding, Hugo, OK

FIG. 39

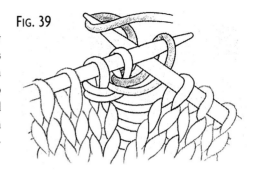

EASY BOBBLES

I crochet, rather than knit, bobbles in my sweaters. I yarn over onto the hook to start and make five double crochets in the bobble stitch, holding back one loop of each on the hook. I pull the yarn through all the loops on the hook, then replace the stitch on the knitting needle, pushing the bobble through to the correct side. I find the results identical to knitted bobbles, and the work need not be turned.
—*Catherine Ham, Austin, TX*

WISP KNITTING

Knitters can produce the same plush, textured rugs, wall hangings, and pillows that are produced by latch hookers. This simple technique is for those who prefer working with a pliable yarn backing rather than a rigid canvas; who like to use up their yarn scraps; who enjoy watching their work grow, rather than "counting down" rows on a canvas; and who are happy to move on to another project when the first is complete, without binding, sizing, and finishing.

The wisps are cut lengths of yarn that are tied onto the yarn before it is knit. The wisps may be any length, and depending on the yarn weight, they may be single or double strands (attached separately). Before buying materials, make a sample to learn the technique and determine if the wisps should be single or double. The basic stitch is worked in worsted yarn for wall hangings and pillows, and in heavier yarn to provide body and strength for rugs.

To make the sample, use worsted yarn and size 8 needles. To master the stitch, work the first section without attaching wisps. Cast on 15 sts. *Row 1:* Purl across the row. *Row 2:* K1; *yarn forward, sl1, yarn back; k1. Repeat from * across row. *Row 3:* Purl across row. *Row 4:* With yarn forward, sl1, yarn back; *k1; yarn forward, sl1, yarn back, repeat from * across row. Continue for 9 rows. Look at your work to determine the pattern of the slipped stitches.

Row 10: Now you'll begin tying wisps onto the base yarn at the beginning of each row. Tie on 7 wisps (in general, tie on enough to work a whole row), as follows: Double the wisp strand, and bring the two cut ends around the base yarn and through the looped end. Pull on the two ends to form a half-hitch knot. Follow the instructions for Row 2, slip a wisp into place after each yarn forward, slip the next stitch, and lock the wisp into place with a yarn back; then k1.

Continue in the pattern. Use 8 wisps on the next knit row and alternate between 7 and 8 until the sample is square. Bind off on a purl row.

The needle, yarn size, and tension help determine the proper wisp spacing. To determine spacing, work a row with wisps. Then rip it and measure the distance between them. Use this to guide your spacing when tying on wisps.

Once you master the wisp-stitch technique, you can use it for any knit item. You must make allowances for the gauge of the base stitch when you are "grafting" wisps to a knit pattern, but usually the wisp stitch can be used for many practical, decorative items without pattern changes.
—*Margaret S. Peterson, Marshfield, WI*

PICKING UP A DROPPED STITCH

Dropping a stitch is often unintentional, although there are a couple of interesting pattern stitches that rely on dropped stitches for their effect, such as needle weaving when combined with knitting. If you've accidentally dropped a stitch in the row you're currently knitting, rip out the stitches until you get back to the dropped offender. Carefully move the old stitches back to the left needle so they are correctly positioned and match the other stitches on that needle (see Fig. 40A). Pick up the dropped stitch, position it on the left needle like the other stitches, and work the stitch.

If you dropped a stitch several rows below the one you're currently working, a ladder will have

FIG. 40A

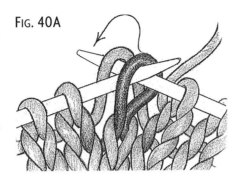

FIG. 40B

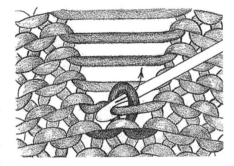

FIG. 40C

formed. Use a crochet hook to work the stitch up the ladder, rung by rung. To correct a knit stitch, insert the hook into the stitch from the front (see Fig. 40B); to correct a purl stitch, insert the hook into the stitch from the back (see Fig. 40C). When you reach the top row, correctly position the stitch on the left needle to knit or purl.

PICKING UP LOOSE STITCHES

Knitters often need to pick up loose stitches. This happens most commonly in hand knitting because you've dropped a few stitches or have taken the work off the needles to rip (unravel) several rows. Machine knitters often rip out a waste yarn machine cast-on to free the bottom-edge stitches and complete a sweater by hand.

If you plan to start knitting with a new ball of yarn, you can pick up with either the knit or purl side facing you. Slip the needle into the loose loops from right to left and back to front, as shown in Fig. 41A. The first row will be worked on the other side. However, if you're picking up after ripping a few rows, and the tip of the left needle needs to end up at the right-hand edge, where the ball is already attached, slip the needle in from left to right and front to back so the last stitch you pick up is at the ball. You can pick up with either the knit or purl side facing you, and your first row will be on the same side.

Your goal is always to pick up the stitches so they aren't twisted because if you knit a twisted stitch in the normal manner, it will be tighter than the other stitches and, being crossed at the bottom, it will look different.

Fig. 41A

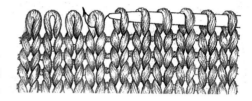

Fig. 41B

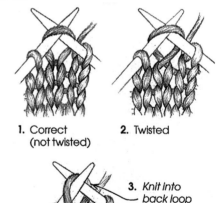

1. Correct (not twisted) **2.** Twisted

3. Knit into back loop to untwist stitch.

Determining whether the loops are twisted or not is easy: The stitch is *untwisted* on the left-hand needle if it opens wide when you insert the right-hand needle to knit or purl (see drawing 1 of Fig. 41B). But if it crosses at the base when you insert the righthand needle into it (drawing 2, Fig. 41B), it was picked up backward (*twisted*). Replace it on the left-hand needle (LHN), or knit it by passing the RHN through the half of the stitch loop on the back side of the LHN (drawing 3, Fig. 41B) to untwist it.

PICKING UP STITCHES

Pick up stitches for attaching a knitted cord such as I-cord by inserting the pick-up needle through both sides of a stitch in a column and pulling a loop through, as shown in Fig. 42. Repeat, working down the column, for the desired number of stitches.

KNITTING REPAIR HINT

To hold a knitted garment securely when picking up dropped stitches or mending a hole, place the section to be worked on a clean hairbrush.

—*Kathleen C. Saxe, Sioux City, IA*

RIPPING STOCKINETTE STITCH

To rip back many rows in stockinette stitch, take a thinner needle and run it under the front leg of every stitch on the row below the mistake, as shown in Fig. 43. Then just rip away. The ripping stops when you get to the needle, and all the stitches are set correctly so you can resume knitting after transferring them to the right size needle. Since I always use circular needles, either end is ready to knit.

—*Peg Boren, McAllen, TX*

FIG. 42

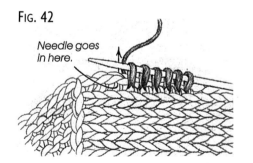

Needle goes in here.

FIG. 43

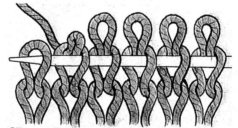

Slip needle through front leg of each stitch on row so ripping will stop with stitches aligned.

Short Rows

Knitting short rows is a nearly invisible method of shaping a knitted piece. A short row is any portion of the row less than a full row. Whether knitting by hand or machine, short rows are always worked in pairs. To work short rows by hand, you simply stop partway in a row, turn the work, and purl back over that section, then turn again and continue knitting, as shown in Fig. 44A. By machine, the process is the same: Select the needles you want to knit using the hold position or pushers, knit a partial row, then knit back on the same stitches, and continue knitting.

If you place extra rows in the middle of a section of knitting, making each short row a little longer than the previous one until you're knitting full rows, you'll cause the fabric to bulge outward or curve downward. Short rows can be used to construct seamless darts, sock heels, mitered corners, spheres, ruffles, or gathers.

The only problem with knitting short rows is that holes can form at the turn. There are two ways to prevent these holes. The first is to decrease the total stitch count at the turn by knitting or purling two stitches together.

The second method, which maintains the stitch count, is to wrap the yarn around the stitch after the turn. Fig. 44B shows how to wrap the yarn when knitting by hand. Work to the turn, slip the next stitch from the left to right needle as if to purl, bring the yarn to the

front (for knitting) or back (for purling), and then slip the stitch back to the left-hand needle. Return the yarn to the other side, turn, and work the short row, starting at the first stitch on the left-hand needle. When you are ready to work the wrapped stitch, scoop the wrap up with the stitch, reposition the left needle, and work the two together.

Fig. 44A

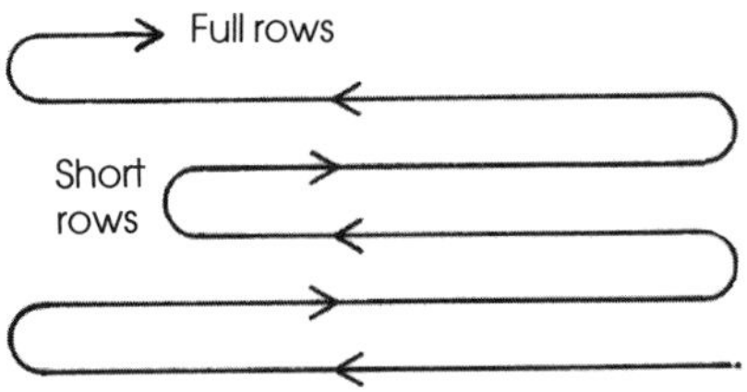

Full rows

Short rows

Fig. 44B

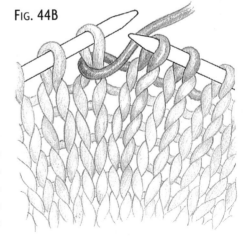

If you're machine knitting, wrapping the yarn is even easier. After you knit the short row and are ready to knit back, place the yarn into the hook of the next needle after the short row, then knit back. On a subsequent row, the extra loop of yarn will be knitted with the stitch on that needle, preventing a hole from forming at the turning point.

KNITTING BACKWARDS

Knitting backwards is helpful when you're knitting narrow areas, bobbles, or short rows, which would otherwise require frequent turning of the work back and forth to knit the right side and purl the wrong side. When knitting backwards, you can knit faster by working every row from the right side, without turning at the end of a row. Knitting backwards also makes it easier to follow a graphed design, because you don't have to reverse every other row of the graph, as you would if purling from the wrong side.

To knit backwards at the end of a knit row and keep the stitches untwisted and properly oriented for the next knit row, insert the left-hand needle from front to back into the first stitch on the right-hand needle. Wrap the yarn from left to right over the left-hand needle, and pull the wrap through the loop, as shown in Fig. 45. Alternate a row of forward and a row of backward knitting as needed to complete the required section.

THIMBLES FOR KNITTERS

Knitting small stitches on small, sharp needles? Slip on a leather quilting thimble. It protects fingertips while maintaining feel and flexibility.
—Margaret Rauhut, Chicago, IL

FIG. 45

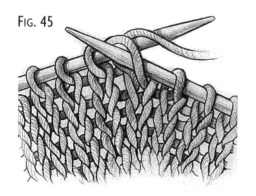

Chapter 3

MULTICOLOR KNITTING

Two-color knitting

To knit with two colors on a row, there are several techniques for holding the yarns. Here is a method in which both colors are held in the same hand: The first strand (A) is held in the right hand as if you were knitting with it alone, with the yarn passing over the index finger and under the palm of the hand. The second strand (B), closest to you, is held between the thumb and the index or middle finger and also passes under the palm.

As you knit, throw whichever color is called for in the pattern. To throw A, raise your index finger and wrap the needle, as shown in Fig. 46A. To throw B, rotate your hand clockwise so that the palm is more visible, and pick up B with your index finger so you can wrap the needle (Fig. 46B). For even knitting, always hold the same color in the same position in your hand.

Stranded weaving

Stranded weaving is a way to carry a yarn at the back when knitting Fair Isle or stranded knitting, without creating long floats between areas of the same color. It's basically the same technique as that used to finish yarn ends, described on p. 44. You simply twist the two yarns together every two or three stitches, using a loose, even tension.

FIG. 46A

FIG. 46B

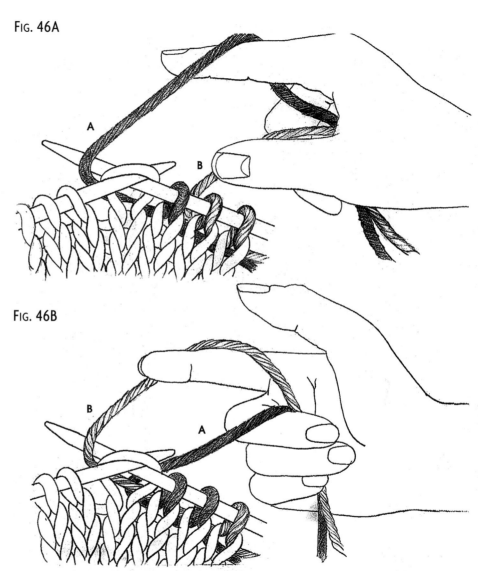

TWO-HANDED TWO-COLOR KNITTING

I have always used and taught the "two-fisted" system of stranded knitting, with one color held in each hand, the right-hand color thrown American style, and the left-hand color picked in the Continental way. This is wonderfully rhythmic and easy to do, on the *knit* side. Even weaving in of either color to avoid long floats is quickly learned. However, American-style knitters have a terrible time purling with the left hand, and we end up with a tangled mess of yarn and uneven knitting when we do stranded knitting in the flat.

The solution is to put one color around the neck. From the knitting, the yarn goes over the left shoulder, around the neck, and down over the right shoulder. The right-hand color is purled with the right hand as usual. When the left color is called for, you just flip it over the needle with the left thumb, as shown in the left-hand drawing of Fig. 47. I seldom have a tension

FIG. 47

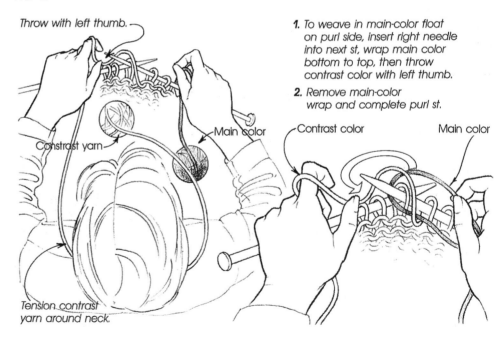

Throw with left thumb.

Contrast yarn

Main color

Tension contrast yarn around neck.

1. To weave in main-color float on purl side, insert right needle into next st, wrap main color bottom to top, then throw contrast color with left thumb.

2. Remove main-color wrap and complete purl st.

Contrast color

Main color

problem, but with a slippery yarn it is easy to loop the yarn through the fingers of the right hand. Moving your head back or lowering your hands can counteract left-hand slack.

To weave in the contrast color, if the main color is needed for more than three or four stitches, *hold the contrast yarn up with the thumb and purl one stitch with the main color under it.* Work the next few stitches as usual with the right hand, and the yarn will naturally be thrown over the neck yarn.

If the pattern calls for a run of contrast color, weave in the main color by purling with the contrast color and the flip method for two stitches. *Then put the needle in the next stitch, and wrap the right-hand yarn from bottom to top. Do not purl the stitch, just wrap. Flip the left yarn as usual.* Remove the right-hand wrap, as shown in the right-hand drawing of Fig. 47, and complete the stitch.

I have found that I can purl Fair Isle work using this method just as fast and smoothly as I can knit it—not counting the time it takes to explain what I'm doing to amused bystanders.
—*Sandy Terp, Phillipsburg, NJ*

BACK-AND-FORTH KNITTING

The simplest Fair Isle patterns require working simultaneously with two balls of yarn. Argyle and complex contemporary patterns may require several balls.

The secret to changing colors in the middle of a row without leaving a hole in the work is to tightly twist the new yarn around the old. Sounds great. But this simple twist at every color change, coupled with turning the work around at the end of a row, quickly makes a mess of strands that would cause Arachne to shudder!

The solution is to knit back and forth on the same side of the fabric, no matter what kind of stitch you're making. (This technique is also useful when you're making a large, heavy, or bulky item that is difficult to turn after every row.)

To visualize the technique, loosely knit about 1 in. of a 20-stitch stockinette swatch, changing colors in the row. When you get to the end of a knit row, stop. In stockinette, you'd normally turn the work to purl the back. But purling is simply knitting on the wrong side, so, although you'll be working on the front side of the fabric, you'll be making the same stitch you'd be making if you were purling on the back side. You'll be working from the left edge of the fabric to the right, instead of from right to left.

Insert the left-needle tip into the back of the first stitch on the right needle, slipping the left needle behind the right. (To check the needle's position, turn your work around and insert the needle as if to purl; then look at it on the wrong side.) Wrap the working yarn around the left-needle tip counterclockwise (see Fig. 48), and pull the left-needle tip through the space underneath the right needle to form the stitch.

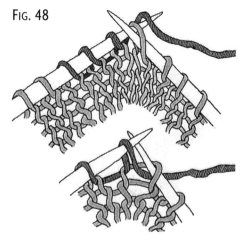

FIG. 48

When knitting from left needle to right, the twists at the color changes are all counterclockwise. When you knit back across the row, from right needle to left, the color changes are twisted clockwise. By the time you get to the end of the row, all of your yarns are untangled and ready to go again for the next row.

—Shelley Cypher, Laguna Niguel, CA

MANAGING TWISTED KNITTING YARNS

Instructions for multicolor knitting usually tell you to pick up a new color from *under* the old color, which twists the yarns. If your colors are wound onto bobbins, and you're working back and forth on two needles, the strands are not hard to untwist. However, I prefer to work straight from the ball and in the round, so the yarns twist more and more as I work. As soon as the twists become awkward, I start picking up the new color from *over* the old color, and the yarns start to untwist. When the yarns are fully untwisted, I switch back to picking up under the old color, and the problem takes care of itself.

I also put the balls of yarn into a bag or box a few feet away from me. This seems to extend the amount of time I can twist the yarns in one direction.

—Debbie Ott, Glenella, MB, Canada

HIGH-SPEED FAIR ISLE

Many knitters are attracted to multicolored patterns in which the unused yarns are stranded behind the work (Fair Isle is the best-known example), but they are discouraged by the slow pace of the work when changing colors repeatedly across each row. Here's a speedy alternative to the typical process: Using either circular or double-pointed needles, work across the row, knitting every stitch that should be in color A and slipping (as if to purl) every stitch that should be in color B, which you can ignore for the time being. At the end of the row and without turning, slide the stitches back to the right-hand point of the needle, pick up color B, drop A, and work every stitch that should be B, slipping every stitch that was previously worked in A. Now you can turn and work the same way on the purl side. If you're working in the round, knit one round with A then one round with B to complete each single row. Besides providing a considerable increase in speed, you'll find this method makes it easier than usual to control the tension of the strands, avoiding gathered, rippling fabric. After you slip a group of stitches, stretch them out smoothly on the right-hand needle before stranding the yarn past to the next stitch. This will measure out just the right amount of yarn for that strand.

—June Hemmons Hiatt, San Francisco, CA

EVEN GAUGE WITH COLOR KNITTING

In knitting a two- or three-color pattern, I find that I get a much more even finished gauge if I use a needle one size larger on the multicolor rows than on the single-color rows that occur periodically in the design.

—*Betsy Carpenter, Los Altos, CA*

REVERSIBLE SWEATERS

I love to make many-colored sweaters inspired by Kaffe Fassett, and have recognized that the inside is often as attractive, in a handwoven sort of way, as the outside. So I've started making reversible sweaters. The two sides look very different, so I feel like I get two sweaters instead of one.

To make the sweater reversible, I knit with floats that extend all the way to the selvage, even when that isn't necessary to the "front" pattern. I weave in the ends carefully, join neatly, and make ribbings or hems that are attractive on the back as well as the front. Pockets in the side seams are no problem at all; they just turn inside out.

To make the buttons reversible, I knit buttonholes on both sides of the front. Then I sew the buttons to a length of grosgrain ribbon and but-ton them through the side where they would usually be sewn. Then I can button the other side over them. When I turn the sweater inside out, I just unbutton the ribbon and button it through the other side, which also makes the sweater unisex.

—*Lynn Derus, Atlanta, GA*

JOINING A NEW COLOR

When working colorwork patterns, join new colors at the edge by tying a loop in the new yarn. Slip the old yarn through the loop, and pull the new yarn firmly up against the edge of the swatch (see Fig. 49). Then tie a square knot with the two ends. This may seem thick, but it prevents the ends from loosening, even if the yarns are slippery.

FIG. 49

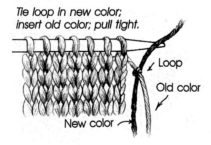

Tie loop in new color;
insert old color; pull tight.

Loop

Old color

New color

FIG. 50

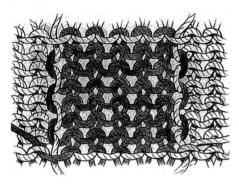

FIG. 51

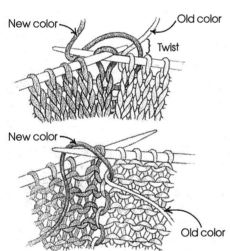

New color — — Old color

Twist

New color —

New color —

Old color

INTARSIA KNITTING

Knitting with the intarsia method is one way to knit with several colors. Unlike stranded knitting, where the colors are knitted in frequently along the row and carried across the back of the fabric when not in use, the colors in intarsia knitting generally appear at isolated spots along the row, as shown in Fig. 50, and each color of yarn is left hanging until needed in the next row, when it's picked up and knitted. Intarsia produces a single thickness of fabric, whereas stranded knitting creates a double- or triple-thick fabric, depending on the number of colors that are used.

Twist yarns at the color change when you're knitting intarsia or argyle to prevent holes from forming between colors. Whether knitting or purling, the new color yarn is always positioned to the right of the old color yarn. Drop the color you've just finished, and with your right hand, reach under it for the new color, as shown in Fig. 51. If the new color is already to the right of the old color, i.e., you've knit past it with the color you're about to drop, just knit or purl without twisting. It will automatically cross over the color change place, so no hole will form.

If you forget to twist on the one-stitch cross-hatching in argyle knitting, the crosshatched stitches will be crossed rather than flat.

To add a new color in intarsia and finish the yarn end at the same time, twist in the new yarn with the three stitches just before the new yarn is needed. Hold the new color yarn at the back of the work and wrap the yarns together between each of the three stitches before the color change, as shown in Fig. 52. To keep tangling to a minimum, alternate the direction of the twist on adjacent stitches.

FIG. 52

First twist color a over b, then b over a

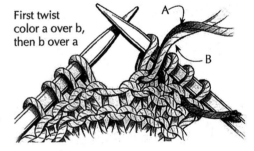

A

B

PURL DUPLICATE STITCH

Purl duplicate stitch is a very neat and secure method for weaving in the many ends of yarn that result with intarsia (knitting with many yarn colors in short pieces). Working on the wrong side, thread the colored yarn end onto a tapestry needle. Then insert the needle into the closest adjacent purl bump along the lower half of the same row as the colored stitch from which the tail exits, going away from the colored stitches (see Fig. 53). This bump curves downward, like a frown. Follow the thread path and insert the needle into the bump just above; this stitch is connected to the edge colored stitch. It curves up like a smile. Weave under about four pairs of purl bumps always going through each twice and moving away from the intarsia block to close up the hole between colors.

FIG. 53

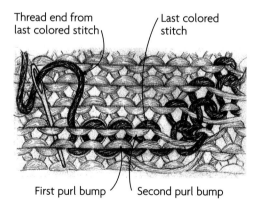

Thread end from last colored stitch

Last colored stitch

First purl bump

Second purl bump

UNTANGLING YARN BOBBINS

When you knit with different color yarns on bobbins, they often get tangled. Here's a way to avoid the problem: After winding the yarn on a bobbin, slip a piece of a drinking straw over the end of the yarn so the yarn is drawn through the straw while you're knitting.
—Mrs. M. Harrison,
West Vancouver, BC, Canada

NO KNITTING-BOBBIN TANGLE

When using as many as ten bobbins in a row for intarsia, I could never keep the bobbins straight and unsnarled as I went to turn my work. Now I place my needle along the top edge of a free-standing knitting basket, with the completed row face down and the bobbins hanging into the basket. Now it's easy to turn the basket and pick up the needle to do the next row, and the bobbins are in order and untangled.
—Mimi Nelson, Trotwood, OH

SEAMLESS INTARSIA

When *Threads* No. 41 arrived with the article about knitting argyles without seams, I determined to have my next project be a pair of argyle socks. However, I soon discovered an even easier way to knit seamless garments with several colors in intarsia. Multicolor knitting in the round is generally perceived to be impossible because after the first row has been knit around, the yarn for each color change ends up on the wrong side of the color area, instead of at the beginning where you need it for the next row. The solution is to purl every other row as you would with straight needles, always turning at a color change.

In order to keep your knitting a seamless tube while you're working back and forth, you twist the first and last colors together *before* you begin each next row. When you reach the last color area, pass the skein for the color you just finished through the loop made by the initial twist, as shown in Fig. 54. You'll then purl or knit the remaining stitches using yarn from the loop (which of course slides freely in the initial twist), then slide the loop closed at the end of the row.

When the color change is on a diagonal, as in argyles, simply slip a stitch or two at the end of a round in order to maintain the pattern. This technique can be used with as many colors as you like, for virtually any intarsia pattern, including seamless argyle socks.
—*Nancy Larson, Knoxville, TN*

FIG. 54

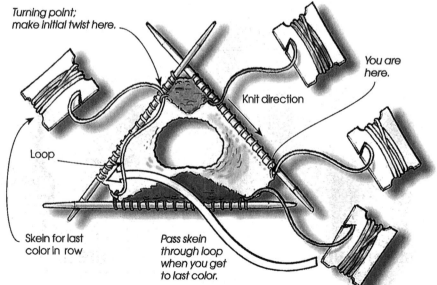

Turning point; make initial twist here.

You are here.

Knit direction

Loop

Skein for last color in row

Pass skein through loop when you get to last color.

VARIEGATED YARNS

A variegated yarn changes colors along its length. The colors can be the result of blending, dyeing, or printing. An advantage to knitting with a variegated yarn is that you can change colors without switching yarns, thus avoiding yarn ends.

Often the colors in variegated yarn appear sequentially at regular intervals on the strand. When knitting a narrow area with such yarn, the colors may shade gradually from one to the next. By contrast, in a wide section, the colors may appear jumbled, like in a tweed. You can experiment on swatches to explore the options for different effects.

VARIEGATED KNITTING

Variegated yarns knit up in patches of color instead of in the soft, heathery look the skeins had. And the design of the patches can change drastically when you knit a sleeve or cardigan front, for example, because of the change in the width of the knitting. To minimize the patching, knit two rows from one ball of yarn, then two rows from another, then two rows from the first, and so on. You'll have short yarn floats at the edge, but the colors will be more evenly distributed.
—*Ruth Galpin, Southport, CT*

RESCUING MIXED-DYE-LOT YARNS

A non-knitter friend recently bought me several skeins of yarn in a closeout sale she attended. Because she didn't know about the importance of dye lots, no two skeins were from the same lot. But I made a beautiful sweater from them by knitting and purling rows 1 and 2 from one skein and attaching a second skein for rows 3 and 4. I continued to alternate skeins every two rows. The skeins from the different dye lots made the yarns appear slightly variegated. The sweater turned out lovely, and I made good use of all the yarn.
—*Judith Nyman-Schaaf, Seattle, WA*

ONE-ROW STRIPES IN FLAT KNITTING

When you want to randomize the patches produced by variegated yarn or different dye lots, use up assorted colors, or change gradually from one color to another; knit with three balls of yarn, changing yarns at the end of every row. The floats of yarn will be short and inconspicuous, and both edges will be the same. Three closely related colors in garter stitch give a tweed effect. Two balls of the main color and one ball of a contrast color worked in hopsac, or woven, stitch produce polka dots (see Fig. 55). You work hopsac stitch on an odd number of stitches, repeating two rows as follows:
Row 1: K1, *sl1 purlwise with yarn in front, k1*, rep to end of row.
Row 2: P2, *sl1 purlwise with yarn in back, p1*, rep to end of row.
—*Joy Beeson, Voorheesville, NY*

FIG. 55

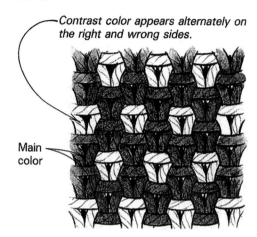

Contrast color appears alternately on the right and wrong sides.

Main color

FIG. 56

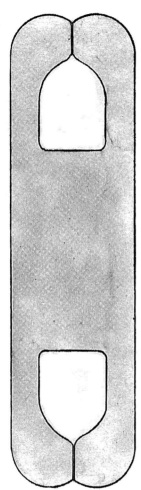

HOMEMADE YARN BOBBINS

Recently I started a project that called for about 20 large knitting bobbins. It was inconvenient to go shopping, and it would have been expensive, so I improvised by using a few old, warped plastic food-storage containers and lids. I drew a pattern (shown full size in Fig. 56), traced it onto the plastic, and cut the bobbins out. They turned out to be better in every way than commercial bobbins: nonbrittle, inexpensive, and satisfying!

—*Gloria Albert, Shaker Heights, OH*

BLENDED COLOR EFFECT

You can achieve a blended color effect by knitting alternate stitches in two shades of the same color. For example, suppose you are making a strip coat and you cannot find exactly the shade of green you want for the solid-color sections. But by knitting two different greens—a yellowy green and a blue green—alternating one stitch of each, the result is a new shade in between. Reverse the position of the colors on each succeeding row to prevent vertical stripes. Alternate the colors by carrying the non-knitting color behind the knitting color every stitch. This creates a subtle texture.

YARN BUTTERFLIES

A yarn butterfly is useful whenever you need small lengths of yarn such as for argyle knitting. The butterfly is a tiny center-pull skein that keeps the yarn out of your way when it's not in use. Place the yarn around your thumb so that the end dangles in your palm. Then wind as much yarn as you think you'll need in a figure-eight between your thumb and little finger, as shown in the left-hand drawing of Fig. 57. To secure the butterfly, tie the final end around the center of the bundle in two or three half hitches, as shown in the right-hand drawing. Weave or knit from the end that dangled in your palm. If the butterfly loosens too much as you use the yarn, retie the half hitches.

FIG. 57

LOW-COST DURABLE YARN BOBBINS

A good bobbin for weaving or knitting yarns is hard to find. I make my own from plastic needlepoint canvas, as shown in Fig. 58. I find the 2-in. by 4-in. size most useful, and anything larger than 4 in. not really firm enough to work with. After cutting, I smooth the plastic with an emery board.

—*Carol Hiebert, Downs, IL*

FIG. 58

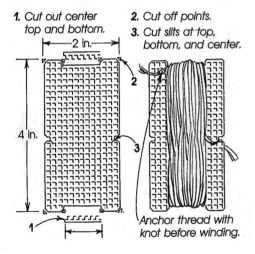

1. Cut out center top and bottom.

2. Cut off points.
3. Cut slits at top, bottom, and center.

2 in.

4 in.

1

Anchor thread with knot before winding.

A SLICK BOBBIN FOR HAND KNITTERS

Machine knitters have a notion that I've never seen in a shop or catalog for hand knitters. It's a plastic yarn bobbin that snaps closed and greatly improves on traditional hand-wound bobbins for ease of winding and unwinding, protection of the yarn, and portability. The disc-shaped bobbin looks like a yo-yo, as shown in Fig. 59, but one side pops open to reveal the central core you wrap your yarn around. The side snaps shut to cover the yarn and secure the working end. You can easily unwind more yarn without opening the bobbin up. The bobbins come in three sizes, called Easy Bob (1⅛ in. diameter), Big Bob (3½ in.), and Giant Bob (6 in.), and all are inexpensive; ten Easy Bobs are less than $3. These things are great for intarsia knitters and those who travel. They're available by mail from Kruh Knits; call (800) 248-KNIT.

—*Hannelore Ring, San Diego, CA*

FIG. 59

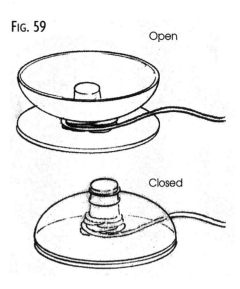

Open

Closed

Chapter 4

GARMENTMAKING TIPS

MAKING SWEATER "MUSLINS"

Before starting a sweater in a pattern I've never made, I make a "muslin," or test garment, in inexpensive knit yardage. I use the measurements given in the pattern to make a paper pattern, then serge an inexpensive model of the garment to check the size and drape. Then, armed with my gauge swatch and the model sweater, I can easily adjust the pattern before casting on a single stitch.

—Nan D. Carlson, Newark, NY

KNITWEAR DESIGN WITH THE AID OF A PHOTOCOPIER

For an inexpensive knitwear design tool, I draw a basic drop-shoulder sweater shape on a sheet of paper, then photocopy it onto 8½-by-11-in. overhead transparency film using the copier's bypass/hand-feed option. (Transparency film for copiers is available at stationery stores and photocopy shops.) I then lay transparencies over interesting fabrics, prints, and textures to look for design inspirations. The transparencies go with me to fabric stores, flea markets, gardens, or museums—anyplace where ideas are likely to present themselves. I also make lots of plain white paper copies and use a large collection of colored markers to play with color ideas and details before beginning the final graphing process.

—Jana Trent, Colleyville, TX

CALCULATING STITCHES

To calculate how many stitches you'll need for a given section of a sweater, start by measuring your gauge swatch to learn the stitch and row gauge. Measure and mark an area 4 in. wide and 4 in. long on your swatch, preferably at the center. Count the number of stitches (horizontally) and rows (vertically) in this area, and divide by 4. This yields the number of stitches or rows you have per inch.

To calculate how many stitches and rows you'll need for a section of knitting, multiply your gauge (sts/in. and rows/in.) by the width and length of the sweater section. For example, if the section measures 20 in. wide and your stitch gauge is 5 sts/in., then: 20 in. x 5 sts/in. = 100 sts. If your section measures 10 in. long and your row gauge is 7 sts per in., then: 10 in. x 7 rows/in. = 70 rows. So casting on 100 sts and knitting for 70 rows will result in a section that's 20 in. wide and 10 in. long.

A RIBBING BAND KNIT ALONG WITH A SWEATER

Knitting the ribbing band of a cardigan at the same time as the body is a great idea. Unfortunately, ribbing stretches more than stockinette stitch and will sag if it is knit at the same gauge, but who wants to change gauge mid-row?

Here's what I do. About every 3 in. or 4 in., I knit a short row on the body of the sweater: I knit across the body of the sweater up to the ribbing, turn, slip the first stitch, and continue back across the body. On the next row, I continue all the way across the ribbing. This keeps the ribbing shorter and eliminates sagging.

—*Jean Dickinson, Williamstown, VT*

KNITTING TWO PIECES AT ONCE

I prefer to knit both cardigan sweater fronts at the same time. To keep the two balls of yarn from tangling, I put each in a soup bowl on the floor.

—*Ann Ingraham, Eureka, CA*

KNIT BUTTONHOLES YOU WON'T MIND SEEING

I like to handsew around the buttonholes in my hand knits. If I'm using a 3- or 4-ply yarn, I separate the plies and use one or two plies to do buttonhole stitch around the buttonhole. This makes a really neat buttonhole, which I whip shut until the sweater is blocked. I also use the one or two plies to sew the button on.

—*Elizabeth Custer, Creston, IA*

PERFECT PLACEMENT FOR KNIT BUTTONHOLES

In published sweater patterns, horizontal buttonholes are invariably placed dead center on the buttonhole band. If you sew the button in the center of the button band, the closed garment will reveal the inner edge of the button band because the buttonholes are always under stress when the buttons are done up (see the top drawing of Fig. 60). The larger the button and buttonhole, the more the button band will show. Sewing the button toward the inside of the band allows the borders to lie correctly but makes the button appear off center.

FIG. 60

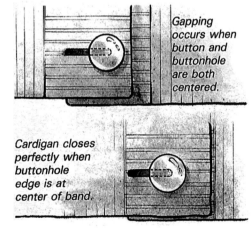

Gapping occurs when button and buttonhole are both centered.

Cardigan closes perfectly when buttonhole edge is at center of band.

To make the two borders lie properly aligned and the button appear in the center of the band, offset the buttonhole so its outer edge is the center stitch of the buttonhole band. Then sew the button in the center of its band. The closed button will appear in the center of the border, and the borders will lie correctly (see the bottom drawing of Fig. 60).
—*The Right Reverend Richard Rutt, Bishop of Leicester, Leicester, England*

KNIT BUTTONHOLES FOR GIRLS OR BOYS

I knitted a sweater with the buttonholes on both fronts for a yet-to-be-born baby. When the baby is born, the buttons can be sewn on the appropriate side, closing the hole beneath. If the sweater is passed on to another child or sibling of the opposite sex, the buttons can be transferred easily to the other side.
—*Marion E. Scoular, Duluth, GA*

INVISIBLE BUTTONHOLES

Hiding a sweater's buttonholes in the purl part of a k1, p1 rib can be very effective. This is the method I use. When I'm ready to knit the first buttonhole, I work half the rib stitches, ending on a knit stitch as seen from the front. Using a separate piece of yarn, I work the last half of the rib stitches and continue to work each side of the buttonhole with separate yarn until it's the right length. Then I drop the added strand and work all the way across the ribbing with the original skein. I carry the extra strand by twisting it loosely in the back when I'm ribbing from the right side. On the wrong side of the work, I ignore it.

I carry the strand up this way until I come to the next buttonhole. If the strand runs out, I work in another, as I did at the beginning. This is as invisible a knit buttonhole as I've ever seen.
—*Alice Smock, Mercer Island, WA*

MAKING DORSET BUTTONS

Dorset buttons provide a beautiful finishing touch for special knitted, crocheted, or sewn garments. They are made by embroidering a single length of thread over and around a suitably sized ring. You can use any type of thread, from fine embroidery silk to knitting yarn. For the ring choose smooth metal, bone, or plastic in the desired size.

Use a blunt tapestry needle for working the button, but change to a sharp one for finishing if you prefer. You must begin with a very long thread as you cannot join more thread until you start covering the spokes. Tie the thread to the ring, hold the loose end behind the ring, and work the first six or seven buttonhole stitches over it. Cut off any excess thread tail.

FIG. 61

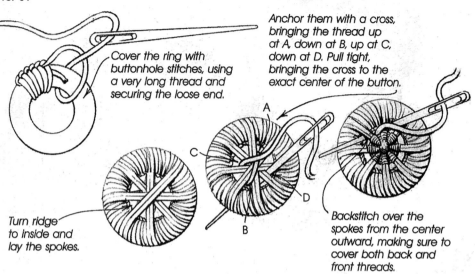

Cover the ring with buttonhole stitches, using a very long thread and securing the loose end.

Anchor them with a cross, bringing the thread up at A, down at B, up at C, down at D. Pull tight, bringing the cross to the exact center of the button.

Turn ridge to inside and lay the spokes.

Backstitch over the spokes from the center outward, making sure to cover both back and front threads.

Cast the button by covering the ring with buttonhole stitches, as shown in Fig. 61, keeping them tight and close together so the ring doesn't show through. Slip your needle through the flint stitch so the join is invisible.

Slick by turning all stitches inward so the outside of the ring is smooth and the ridge is on the inside.

With the thread at the back of the ring, lay the spokes of the button by bringing the thread down to the bottom of the ring and then up in front at the exact center. Rotate the ring an eighth turn and wind again from back to front. Continue until you have made eight spokes. Fasten these securely by making a cross in the middle: bring the needle up where the first spoke was made and over the last, and repeat from side to side, keeping the cross exactly in the center of the ring. (The front and back threads will not align until you make the center cross. Don't be alarmed by this.)

To fill, or round, the button, backstitch over each of the spokes, keeping the thread taut and even. Fill in as much as you like, leaving a long thread to sew the button to the garment. You can make a shank for sewing on the button, using a knitting needle as a gauge. If you prefer to round the button using a different color, change threads by working over the new thread at the back for a few stitches, picking up the new color and working over the old for a few stitches. Clip the thread ends.

By arranging the spokes differently, you can make a variety of designs.

Thanks to *Slip Knot*, the official magazine of The Knitting and Crochet Guild, for permission to reprint this tip from their issue No. 47.
—*Lesley Conroy, Bradford, England*

EVEN SLEEVES

I always knit the two fronts of a cardigan or two sleeves at the same time from two balls of yarn. To make sure I knit the same number of rows on each piece, I have to remember not to lay the knitting down with one front or sleeve on each needle. I do this by pinning the pieces together with coil-less safety pins about every two inches as the work progresses. This makes it look more like one piece and helps avoid mistakes.

—*Charlotte Stafford, Chesterland, OH*

KNITTING SLEEVES FROM THE TOP DOWN

I usually knit on a circular needle and pick up and knit the sleeves from the shoulder down. To avoid the fuzziness that can occur from over-handling knit garments, particularly on softer yarns like merino, I fold the sweater neatly and place it in a plastic bag (not cloth), leaving the picked up shoulder stitches available at the opening of the bag. To further secure the bag, you can tie a string around the outside.

—*Barbara Bononno, New York, NY*

KNITTED SLEEVES THAT MATCH

For even sleeves with fewer mistakes, start by working both sleeves on the same needle until the ribbing is completed. Then either work to the first increase or to the end of the first pattern. At this point, begin to knit each sleeve separately, measuring length by rows, patterned rows, or increases. At the armhole decreases, begin working the sleeves together again until finished.

—*Mary Papageorgiou, Madison, CT*

KNITTING SLEEVES BEFORE THE BODY

Knit your sleeves first, not last. That way you can correct a gauge or pattern problem with fewer stitches to rip out. Also, you are guaranteeing that you will end up with a sweater, and not just another vest, as I often have if I get bored after knitting just the body.

—*Beth A. Kollé, Seattle, WA*

EASY SWEATER ARMHOLE FACING

When I knit sleeves in the round for a drop-shoulder sweater, I add an inch to the sweater's sleeve length. When I set the sleeve into the body and sew it, I use the extra inch to cover and bind the cut edge on the body.

—*Beth A. Kollé, Seattle, WA*

FIG. 62

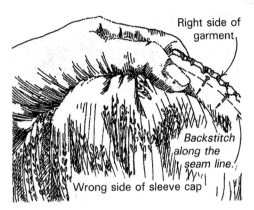

Right side of garment

Backstitch along the seam line.

Wrong side of sleeve cap

SETTING IN KNITTED SLEEVES

Knitters often spoil sweaters when setting in sleeves. For professional-looking set-in sleeves, I use a dressmaking technique: Hold the garment and sleeve at the shoulder seam, right sides together, cupping the sleeve cap over your curved fingers and keeping the two edges together with your thumb (see Fig. 62). Pin closely. Then backstitch, still cupping the cap. To get it perfectly rounded, I ignore the shape of the knit edges. Excess fabric adds welcome bulk under the shoulder, and the cupping distributes the extra fullness evenly. If the cap is too wide to work in evenly, before I sew the sleeve to the shoulder seam I run a piece of yarn through the top of the sleeve to gather it, and sometimes I crochet the edge to firm it.

—*Marne Chandler, Portola Valley, CA*

TAPERED RIBBING

I use tapered ribbing on cuffs that are meant to lie flat. I usually work sleeves from the shoulders down, but if you're working from the bottom up, you can use an invisible cast-on for the sleeves and work the cuff last.

Pick up stitches for the cuff rib, gathering for size, if necessary, in the first row. Knit about two-thirds of the length of the cuff on the size needles you chose for the ribbing. Then change to one size smaller and knit one row. Alternate knitting one row with the ribbing needles and one with the smaller needles a few times to produce a smooth transition. Then rib to the row before the last with the smaller needles. Rib the last row on the ribbing needles; insert the smaller needles—without knitting—and bind off with a tubular method. When using worsted or bulky-weight yarn, I begin the taper about one-third of the way down a 3-in. cuff and change successively to two sizes smaller.

—*Patricia Tongue Edraos, Boston, MA*

DECREASING FOR SLEEVE CUFFS

On a child's sweater I like to eliminate 1½ to 2 in. worth of stitches when I get to the cuff (knitting down from the shoulder), and on an adult's sweater I eliminate up to 3 in. Often when I say this, people worry that the sleeve will have a puffy look, but it doesn't. This much decrease gives you a comfortable sleeve that doesn't pull or drag when worn over a long-sleeved shirt.

—*Jean Baker White, North Haven, ME*

DROP-SHOULDER
SLEEVE SEAMS

My method of inserting drop-shoulder sleeves into the armhole makes a flat, clean, professional-looking seam on all yarns, even bulky cottons. Knit front shoulder seams to back shoulder seams. When the sleeve—knit from the wrist up—is finished, do *not* bind off. Instead, knit three or four rows of stockinette in a contrasting color of the same weight, using scrap yarn. Lay the body of the sweater out flat, right side up. Line up the center of the sleeve, right side down, over the shoulder seam with the edge of the sleeve even with the body selvage and the scrap knitting extending beyond the armhole (see Fig. 63). Pin in place.

Insert a crochet hook, equal to the knitting-needle size, from the top through the first raw sleeve stitch—avoid the scrap yarn that goes into the stitch—and through the selvage stitch on the body edge. With a long length of sweater yarn, pull up a loop through the body selvage and sleeve—one loop on the hook. Insert the hook through the next raw sleeve stitch and body selvage, and draw up another loop—two loops on the hook. Pull the second stitch through first. Continue across the sleeve top, being sure to insert the hook through the raw sleeve stitches so you don't drop any. Unravel and discard the contrast yarn.

—*Karen Hoyle, Excelsior, MN*

FIG. 63

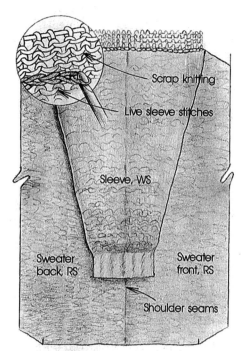

Scrap knitting

Live sleeve stitches

Sleeve, WS

Sweater back, RS

Sweater front, RS

Shoulder seams

After joining front to back at shoulders, center sleeve on shoulder, right sides together, with scrap knitting extending past body selvage. Slip-stitch-crochet all live sleeve stitches to body selvage.

FIG. 64

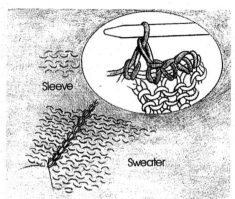

With sleeve and armhole right sides together, pick up and knit a stitch, then another, then bind off the first to set in a sleeve almost invisibly.

BINDING IN A SET-IN SLEEVE

I found the tip for attaching dropped shoulder sleeves (see p. 57) very interesting because I use a somewhat similar method for attaching set-in sleeves. I pin the sleeve to the armhole edge right sides together after joining the shoulder seam. Then from the wrong side using a size 2 needle, I pick up and knit one stitch, then another through both layers at once, just inside the selvages. I bind the first stitch off over the second and continue in this manner around the armhole, as shown in Fig. 64. The result is a knitted seam that makes the two edges blend smoothly on the right side.

—*Laura Jones, Greer, SC*

PREVENT STRETCHED SWEATER SHOULDERS

Oversized sweaters knit with natural fibers often stretch over the shoulders. A handy technique for preventing stretch is to add facing extensions to support the shoulders. I knit the shoulder on both front and back as instructed. When I reach the bind-off row, I knit a turning row of purl. If I'm not working in stockinette, I knit a definite line by ceasing the pattern stitch and working a plain stitch that I can see. After the turning row, I continue knitting in stockinette (see Fig. 65).

For added stability and absolutely no stretch, hand stitch twill tape along the turning row with sewing thread. Sew the facing in place with the yarn tail. Graft the front and back together along the turning rows for an obvious seam, and in the valleys next to the rows for an invisible one. These facings will support the shoulders so that they don't creep downward.

—*Shelly Cypher Springer, San Clemente, CA*

FIG. 65

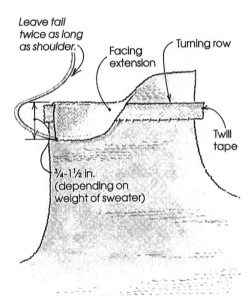

Leave tail twice as long as shoulder.

Facing extension

Turning row

Twill tape

¾–1½ in. (depending on weight of sweater)

BIND OFF AND JOIN PIECES IN ONE STEP

You can knit the back and front pieces together to bind off and join them in one step. Be sure the front and back shoulders have the same number of stitches on the bind-off row. Put matching front and back shoulders on two needles so both points are at the neck or armhole edge. You can hold them right sides together and work from the wrong side to create an invisible join, or hold them wrong side together (working from the right side) to make a decorative ridge on the right side.

Insert a third needle into the first stitch on the front and the first stitch on the back as if they were a single stitch. Knit as shown in Fig. 66; repeat. Bind off whenever there are 2 sts on the RHN by passing the first stitch over the second.

FIG. 66

KNITTED SHOULDER PADS

Knitted shoulder pads can add shape and definition to a knitted garment, such as a sideways-knitted sweater. Ready-made, sewn shoulder pads of foam or batting can be too stiff for a soft sweater, but knitted shoulder pads define the shoulder while remaining flexible. And they're quick and easy to make, since they're basically a simple square of knitting folded diagonally in half.

To make a pad, knit a square 5 to 6 in. wide, using garter stitch (knit every row) for thickness. Fold the square in half and overcast the edges together using the yarn end, as shown in Fig. 67. Try on the garment and place the pad at the shoulder with the long pointed side facing towards the neck and the folded edge along the edge of the shoulder line. Pin the pad in place, then tack it to the sweater with loose stitches at each corner. For thicker pads, use larger needles and a thick, lofty yarn, such as chenille.

FIG. 67

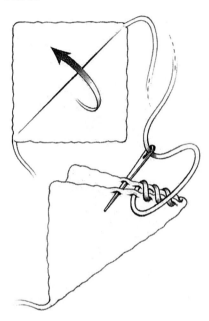

FIG. 68

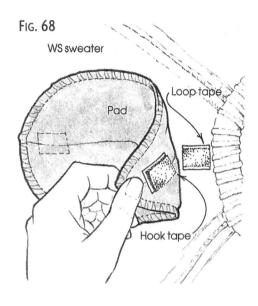

WS sweater

Pad

Loop tape

Hook tape

VELCRO FOR SHOULDER PADS

I have a number of hand-knitted sweaters which improve in appearance with the use of shoulder pads. I thought that foam pads ("no straps or fasteners needed") would do the trick, and to make sure they could never shift or fall out, I attached the pads to the shoulders with small pieces of hook-and-loop (like Velcro). I fastened the hook portion of the tape to the center of the pads with fabric glue and sewed pieces of the loop tape to corresponding places in the sweaters (see Fig. 68). The sweaters fold and store more easily without permanent pads, and I need only one set of pads for all my sweaters.
—*Ruth Neitzel, Merrillville, IN*

RIBBING ON SINGLE-POINTED NEEDLES

Despite all the interest in circular needles and round knitting these days, I still like to use two needles and knit back and forth. Here's my method for knitting ribbing around armholes and necklines with single-pointed needles.

After front and back are complete, I sew one shoulder seam. Starting at one side-seam end of that armhole, I divide the armhole into four sections, two on each side of the shoulder seam. This simplifies distributing the required number of stitches evenly across it. I pick up the stitches and knit on the ribbing I want, then bind off and sew up that side seam, along with the ribbing.

Dividing the neckline in the same way, I pick up the stitches I need, starting at one side of the open shoulder and ending on the other side. I work the ribbing back and forth, bind off, and sew the shoulder and neckband together.

I pick up the stitches on the second armhole the same way as on the first. Then I sew that side seam and ribbing together.
—*Genevieve Smolik, Parma Heights, OH*

PICKING UP NECKLINE STITCHES

When picking up stitches around necklines, especially with fuzzy yarns, I hold the yarn at the back of the work and pick up the stitches with a crochet hook; I put the hook through the stitch at the front, draw the thread through, and place the stitches on a circular needle. This method is very fast and always picks up the correct number of stitches.
—*Freda Jarjoura, Gatineau, PQ, Canada*

NEAT KNIT NECKBAND

For an easy-to-knit neckband that can be bound off and sewn down in one step, try the following method. It works best on a crew neck worked on circular needles, but can also be used for cardigan bands knit horizontally.

Complete the band, keeping all sts on the needle. Turn the neckband to the inside just as you would to sew it down. (A quick way to make the turn easy is to knit one row of purl stitches where the neckband is to be folded to the inside.) Insert right-hand needle (RHN) into the first st, then into the corresponding purl bump at the start of the neckband where sts were first picked up, as shown in Fig. 69. (I find it easier to put five or six of these sweater purl sts back on a smaller double-pointed needle so I can easily find them.) Knit these 2 sts together. *K next st and purl bump tog. Bind off first st on RHN by slipping it over the 2nd st. Repeat from * around neckband. Work loosely to give enough ease for the sweater to slip easily over the head.

—*Diane Zangl, Lomira, WI*

FIG. 69

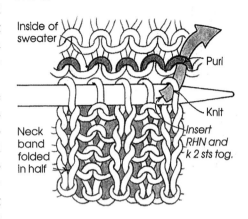

Inside of sweater

Purl

Knit

Insert RHN and k 2 sts tog.

Neck band folded in half

NEAT NECK EDGE PICK-UP

To avoid a loose first stitch when picking up along a neck edge, pick up the first stitch as usual, but pick up the second stitch by yarning over with the working yarn *and* the tail. Besides securing the loose tail, this method also helps you keep tension on the first stitch. Pick up the other stitches as usual. On the next row, work the stitch with two loops as one.

—*Kathe Brinkmann, Urbana, IL*

CROCHET AN EVEN KNIT SELVAGE

Because I knit many fibers and colors into my garments, neck and shoulder selvages are irregular. Before picking up stitches for collars, sleeves, and finishes, I work a row of single crochet into the knit edges, creating an even selvage. I use a firm, medium-tone yarn. Picking up stitches between the single crochet and knit edge is easy, and the new section drapes well.
—*Claire Marcus, Newfoundland, PA*

PICKING UP KNITTING ON FABRIC

My method for picking up knitting stitches along a fabric edge produces a very smooth, even join without pulling the knitting through the fabric. I also use it when I need to pick up stitches along the edge of a knit garment that has been worked with an irregular yarn, such as bouclé or other loopy or bulky fibers.

To join knitting to fabric, embroider a row of even chain stitches along the seamline of the fabric piece. With your knitting needle, pick up a stitch beneath both threads of each chain stitch, as shown in Fig. 70, without going through the fabric. In addition to producing evenly spaced knit stitches, this will fold the seam allowance back to the wrong side. To join knitting to knitting, work the chain stitches close to the edge of the knit piece. This works particularly well when you need a perfect binding for a convex or concave shape.
—*Ilse Altherr, Lancaster, NH*

FIG. 70

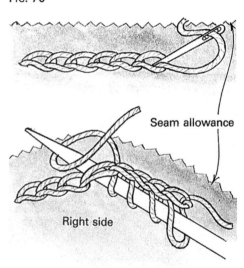

Seam allowance

Right side

Embroider a chain stitch along seam allowance. Insert knitting needle through both loops of chain, pulling knit stitch through.

STEEKS

To create openings for armholes or a front placket on a sweater knitted in the round, you can fill the spaces with steeks, then sew and cut them to open. To make a steek, first knit to where the base of the opening needs to be, and bind off about an inch of stitches, usually about 5 or 7 sts. (You need an odd number of stitches so you'll have a center stitch for cutting.) The bound-off edge serves as a smooth base for later attaching a placket front or sleeve. On the next round, cast on the same number of stitches above the bound-off stitches, by simply twisting backward loops onto the right-hand needle (see Fig. 71). On the following rounds, knit the steek stitches in alternating colors, creating vertical stripes so the cutting line will be easy to see. When you reach the top of the armhole or placket, bind off the steek stitches. Weave in all nearby ends, then baste down the center stitch of the steek in a contrasting color yarn.

Before cutting the steek, machine sew with a medium-length stitch down the center of the stitch on each side of the basted stitch, back-stitching at top and bottom through cast-off and cast-on edges to secure. Carefully cut down the basted center line. After you sew the sleeve into the opening or pick up stitches for a placket opening, tack the edges of the steek to the inside.

IMPROVED STEEK CUTTING

Here's a simple solution to the problem of knit fabric stretching when you're machine stitching along the sides of the steek on a cardigan sweater prior to cutting it. First, hand baste with a contrasting thread up the center-front stitches. Then, turn the sweater inside out and fuse a strip of stabilizer about 2 in. wide up the center (I use Totally Stable by Sulky, available at fabric stores). Next, turn the sweater right side out and cut along the basted line. Not only does the stabilizer keep the front from stretching, it also keeps the edges from raveling while you apply grosgrain ribbon to the front of the cardigan. You can tear off the stabilizer as you apply the ribbon.

—Pamela Costello, Vadnais Heights, MN

FIG. 71

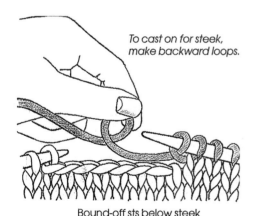

To cast on for steek, make backward loops.

Bound-off sts below steek

SWEATERS IN THE ROUND WITHOUT STEEKS

I like to knit sweaters in the round, but I don't like to use steeks for sleeve openings (the traditional method of knitting in the round over openings), as it takes forever to weave the ends in when finishing. And I don't like to machine-stitch and then cut sleeve openings, because of the gaps and strained stitches where the armhole stops and the sweater begins.

So here's another way. When you reach the row where you want the sleeve opening to begin, knit in your pattern to two stitches before the point where the sleeve opening will begin. Place a marker, and then increase about 1 in. of new stitches over the next 4 sts, and place another marker. Knit around to the point where you want the second sleeve opening, and repeat.

Continue knitting your sweater in the round, knitting the extra stitches every row. If you're using a textured pattern, knit the extra stitches in stockinette stitch. If you're using a multicolor pattern, knit the extra stitches with both colors (k1 red, k1 white, for example).

When you've knitted up to the shoulders, decrease back to the original 4 sts. Graft or purl together your shoulder seams. Now steel yourself, and cut the extra stitches right down the middle, from the shoulder to about 1 in. above where you started the sleeve opening. On circular or double-pointed needles, pick up the sleeve stitches around the opening, ½ in. from the cut edge. The marker stitches will naturally curl in toward the wrong side of the fabric, forming a ½-in. facing. You're ready to knit the sleeve down to the cuff.

I know you won't believe it until you've tried it (I didn't either), but the edges will not unravel. In fact, after a couple of washings, the cut edges will felt and actually become stronger than the knitted fabric.

I didn't invent this technique—it's copied from an old sweater from the north of Norway. I've never tried it with any yarn other than wool, so if you'd like to try it with cotton or man-made fibers, test the yarn you're using by knitting and cutting a tube first.
—*Carol Gordon, Staten Island, NY*

FACINGS INSTEAD OF STEEKS

Here is my method of knitting in the round without steeks. When I come to each underarm, I place 8% of the body stitches on a scrap of yarn (Elizabeth Zimmermann's percentage system). I then cast on the desired number of stitches for the armhole facings, adding a few extra stitches if I'm not using wool, and I continue knitting around.

When I get to the top of the armhole, I bind off the facing stitches and join the shoulder. This gives me a one-piece facing of knit fabric that is not attached at the top or bottom. I machine-stitch two rows down the center of the piece, stretching while stitching so as not to restrict the fabric's give. With wool, this stitching is unnecessary.

Next, I pick up the sleeve stitches around the armhole and the underarm stitches from the holder. I get a nice round armhole, and the sleeve is easy to work. When it's finished, I cut between the two rows of machine stitches to open the armhole. The tiny stitches prevent unraveling, and since I don't have to roll the facing, there is no bulk.

V-NECK IN THE ROUND

When I lived in Norway, I learned to knit sweaters in the round (mostly without patterns). It's hard for me to understand why anyone would go to the trouble of making steeks in circular knitting when you can shape armholes and necklines, even V-necks, without them. Here's one trick I learned for putting a V-neck in a drop-shoulder sweater:

Knit the body of the sweater up to about an inch before the point of your V-to-be. Calculate the number and spacing of stitches needed to decrease on each side of the V.

When you get to the V, decrease as required on both sides of two center-front stitches, but *don't stop knitting in the round.* It will look like you're forming a dart, but trust me, this works. When you get to the shoulder, stop and put all your stitches on a loose string holder with the

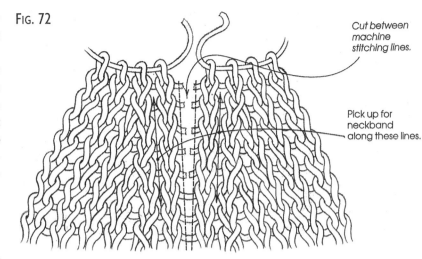

FIG. 72

Cut between machine stitching lines.

Pick up for neckband along these lines.

string ends at the center-front line. Machine stitch two lines with a straight stitch (zigzag stretches the neckline) right down the center between the two center-front stitches to the point of the V. Coat both lines of stitching lightly with Fray Check. When dry, cut between the two lines of machine stitching (see Fig. 72). Now machine stitch and cut your armholes, using Fray Check in the same way. Kitchener stitch the shoulders, then set in and stitch the sleeves. Pick up stitches for your neckband and knit it twice as wide as you want it. Cast off, fold the band to the inside, and hand stitch it over the raw edge. No steeks to weave in, no balls of yarn getting tangled, no yarn waste. *Det var det!* (That's that, in Norwegian).
—*Beth Kollé, Seattle, WA*

SQUARE-HEELED, RIBBED SOCKS

I knit a lot of socks, and find that a k2, p2 rib on the leg and top of the foot fits especially well. Ribbing is stretchy, so I cast on about ⅔ the number of stitches that the stockinette gauge and leg measurement would call for.

I also prefer to knit a "square heel" turn. To turn a square heel, you knit short rows back and forth on the central third of the heel stitches, and at the end of each short row, you knit the last center stitch together with the adjacent side-heel stitch. When you've eliminated all the edge stitches, the center stitches form a right angle to them.

Begin the heel turn by knitting across one-third of the total heel stitches, minus one; k2tog; knit the center third, minus two; k2tog; turn. *Purl the center third, minus one; p2tog; turn. Knit the center third, minus one; k2tog; turn. Repeat from * until exactly one-third of the total heel stitches remain, ending with a wrong-side row.

—*Isobel Morgan, Dubbo, NSW, Australia*

REINFORCING SOCKS

Since I can no longer find nylon heel-and-toe filament, I use silk sewing thread to reinforce the heels and toes of socks when I'm knitting them. It works very well. I also find that I can eliminate stress when turning the corner on gussets by using an extra needle for several rounds. I arrange the stitches with the bottom of the heel on the first needle, one gusset on the second, the instep on the third, and the other gusset on the fourth.

—*Harriet N. Boker, Westerville, OH*

STAY-ON BOOTIES

My booties, shown in Fig. 73, are unusual in that they'll stay on a newborn's feet because of the ribbed construction. I don't know of anyone else who makes them, and since I'm 95, I don't want them to die with me. I knit the booties of Red Heart baby yarn, a three-ply Wintuk, but some of the new washable wool yarns in this size would also work well. They're easiest to knit on a set of five double-pointed needles, size 0, 1, 2, or 3, depending on the gauge you desire; but four needles also work.

Here's how I make them: Cast on 10 sts and knit 18 ridges (36 rows) of garter stitch for the sole. Leave the 10 sts on one needle, and on a second, pick up 10 sts at the cast-on edge. Pick up 18 sts along each side on two more needles— 56 sts in all. Be careful to keep working around in the same direction. Purl 4 rounds, knit 4 rounds, purl 4 rounds, knit 4 rounds, purl 4 rounds.

To shape the toe at one of the 10-st ends, knit and purl short rows back and forth. Work the 10th st together with the closest stitch on the adjacent 18-st needle at the end of each row 16 times (decrease 8 sts per side). You do this by slipping the 10th st to the RH needle purlwise, then back onto the 18-st needle. Knit or purl the first 2 sts on the 18-st needle together. Then turn and work back across the 10 toe sts to the other side.

Now knit around the 40 sts at the ankle for 3 rounds. To prevent a hole at the end of the 1st round, pick up 1 extra st and knit it together with the 1st st on the 2nd round. Make eyelets for the ties on the 4th round: *K2, yo, k2tog* 10 times. Finally, knit 22 rounds, and bind off. Thread crocheted yarn ties or ribbon through the eyelets.

—*Christine Bourquin, Redwood City, CA*

FIG. 73

RIBBON STITCH HOLDER

Recently I knit a hat for my little boy and wanted to try it on him when I'd finished the ribbing. I used a piece of narrow satin ribbon instead of yarn to hold the stitches. Even though my yarn was very fuzzy, the stitches slipped onto the ribbon easily. And having the ribbon to "scoop" against made replacing the stitches on the knitting needles a snap.

—*Ann Miller, Flagstaff, AZ*

GLOVE NEEDLES

While knitting a pair of fine-gauge stranded gloves, I became very frustrated with manipulating four regular-length double-pointed needles. I asked around for glove needles but had no luck. In desperation, I bought a pair of 16-in.-long single-pointed size 0 bamboo needles at a local craft store. I used a mat knife to cut one needle into six 2½-in. segments. Then I shaped points on each end of the short pieces and lightly sprayed my new glove needles with a clear matte finish to prevent the ends from splitting.

The needles were a delight to work with. Because I could easily make a spare, I didn't become frantic over lost needles. When I was done, I stored them in a small plastic box along with the remains of the original needle and bought more bamboo needles in other sizes to cut down for other glove needles.

—*Susan A. Lupton, Indian Hills, CO*

FIG. 74

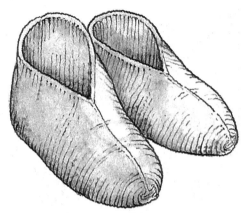

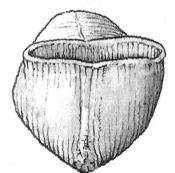

THE WORLD'S SIMPLEST KNITTED SLIPPERS

Make an extra pair or two of these, shown in Fig. 74, for cold winter nights to come. Directions are for women's medium or men's small. For larger sizes, use heavier yarn or larger needles.

Use worsted-weight yarn and size 1, 2, or 3 needles for a firm, tight gauge of about 6 sts and 6 garter ridges (12 rows) per in. Cast on 50 sts, leaving a long end for sewing the heel seam. Work in garter stitch (knit every row), slipping the first stitch of each row for a chain selvage. When the length reaches from the center back of the heel to the end of the little toe, measured along the side of the foot (usually about 8½ in.), begin toe decreases (dec indicates k2tog) on every right-side row as follows:

Row 1: k9, dec, k3, dec, k18, dec, k3, dec, k9.
Row 3: k8, dec, k3, dec, k16, dec, k3, dec, k8.
Row 5: k7, dec, k3, dec, k14, dec, k3, dec, k7.
Row 7: k6, dec, k3, dec, k12, dec, k3, dec, k6.
Row 9: k5, dec, k3, dec, k10, dec, k3, dec, k5.
Row 11: k4, dec, k3, dec, k8, dec, k3, dec, k4.
Row 13: (k3, dec) 2x, k6, (dec, k3) 2x.
Row 15: k2, dec, k3, dec, k4, dec, k3, dec, k2.

Bind off remaining 18 sts. Finish by folding the cast-on edge in half, sewing the back heel seam down to the fold, and tying the last 6 sts all together. Beginning at the toe, sew the side edges together halfway up the instep, leaving enough space to insert your foot. With a separate thread, sew across the toe opening.

Make the second slipper like the first. To be sure they're both the same size, count the garter stitch rows and mark the ridge where the decreases begin, or work both slippers at the same time on the same needle with two separate skeins of yarn.

—Barbara G. Walker, Morristown, NJ

QUICK CORDMAKER

My husband devised an inexpensive, quick cordmaker that I use to make belts, drawstrings, and straps for the garments I handweave. Some basic woodworking skills and a few tools are required to make this gadget. It consists of a plywood disk with eye screws that is attached to the front end of a drill (see Fig. 75). The yarn is attached to the eye screws and to dowels that are clamped to a secure surface. When the drill is turned on, the yarn is wound to make a tight plied cord of any length or thickness.

Decide on the length of your finished cord, multiply that number by 4½ or 5, and cut a guide cord to that length. (Use the yarn you'll use for the finished cord as the guide cord.) Insert the disk's center bolt into the drill-bit socket and attach the dowel clamp to a sturdy piece of furniture. Tie one end of the guide cord to one of the dowels and loop the midpoint of

FIG. 75

Dowel clamp

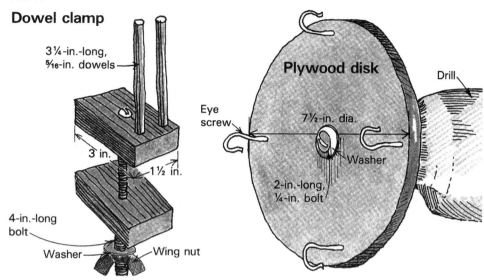

3¼-in.-long, ⁵⁄₁₆-in. dowels

3 in.

1½ in.

Eye screw

Plywood disk

7½-in. dia.

Washer

Drill

2-in.-long, ¼-in. bolt

4-in.-long bolt

Washer

Wing nut

the yarn strand around one of the hooks on the disk. Tie the other end of the strand to the other dowel. This will give you twice the length of the finished cord.

Now hook the yarn for the finished cord around two, three, or four of the eye screws (for a small amount of yarn, I use only two hooks), and wrap it back around the dowels. Continue until you have half the desired thickness of the cord when you squeeze the strands close together. (Note: If you use only two hooks, make sure they are opposite each other in order to keep the winding balanced.)

Run the drill until the yarn is wound tight. Then grab the cord at its center, double it back, and place the disk behind the dowel clamp, keeping the cord taut (have someone help you). Let the cord twist back on itself slowly. Be sure to knot the ends near the dowels before cutting the cord away from the tools. Finished.

—*Jane Taubensee, Bloomington, IN*

KNITTED FINGER PUPPETS

The quickest and cutest knitted toys I've seen can be off your needles and entertaining youngsters in a matter of minutes. They're tiny pull-on hats with faces underneath that just fit your fingertips. Here's the basic recipe (if you enjoy making them, you'll soon find lots of variations): With baby yarn and size 2, 3, or 4 needles, cast on 15 stitches in a color suitable for your character's face. Work stockinette stitch for about ⅝ in. Break the yarn and start again in whatever color you want for the hat, knitting two or three rows in garter stitch, then changing back to stockinette. When the hat measures ½ to ¾ in., cut the yarn, leaving an 8-in. tail. Thread the tail through the 15 stitches, then embroider features onto the center of the face. Pull up the stitches on the thread to close the top, sew up the back seam with the remaining thread, and start another puppet so your little person will have someone to talk to.

—Mimi Nelson, Trotwood, OH

A DOORMAT FROM LARGE-SCALE KNITTING

Here's a method for knitting a durable doormat. You'll need a whole spool (380 ft.) of ³⁄₁₆-in. nylon rope. (Be sure to ask the hardware store for a discount since you're buying the whole spool.) For size 13 knitting needles, cut a 36-in.-long, ⅜-in.-diameter dowel in half. You do not have to make points on the needles. Mark the end of one needle; this needle will be used throughout for all shaping (increasing and decreasing), which occurs on only the right-side rows.

The mat is a bias-knit rectangle, as shown in Fig. 76. Cast on 2 sts with the unmarked needle (this is the WS and from this point on you'll just knit all the stitches of every WS row). Turn to RS. With the marked needle, k1, yarn over (yo), and k1; turn. With unmarked needle, k1, k1 into the back of the yo loop, and k1; turn. With marked needle, k1, yo, k1, yo, and k1. Continue increasing on every RS row until a side of the knitting equals the short side of the desired size mat, using another mat to measure. Then knit the midsection of the mat, increasing with a yarn over after the first stitch and decreasing at the end of every RS row to maintain the same number of stitches in each row. To decrease, knit up to the last 2 sts, slip 1 (sl1) st purlwise, k1, and pass slipped stitch over (psso).

Knit the midsection until the length of the long side equals that of the mat, then begin decreasing at each end of the RS rows as follows: Sl1 purlwise, k1, psso. Knit to the last 2 sts, sl1 purlwise, k1, and psso. Decrease to 3 sts, knit the

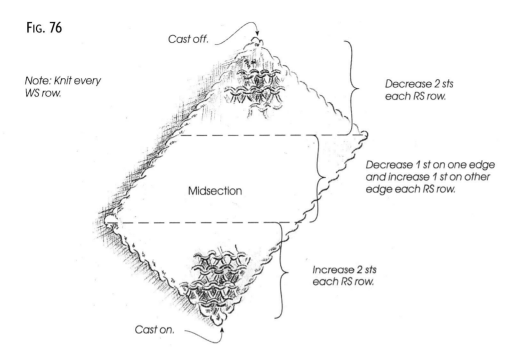

FIG. 76

Cast off.

Note: Knit every WS row.

Decrease 2 sts each RS row.

Midsection

Decrease 1 st on one edge and increase 1 st on other edge each RS row.

Increase 2 sts each RS row.

Cast on.

WS row, decrease to 2 sts (RS row), and cast off. Cut the rope and sear the end with a lit match to prevent fraying. Work in both ends of rope.

The idea to replace my own shredding doormat comes from three sources: Barbara Walker's article on bias knitting in *Threads* No. 4 (pp. 54-55); Dave Fougner's out-of-print booklet *The Manly Art of Knitting* (New York: Scribner's, 1972), wherein he knits a hammock with a rope, using shovel handles for needles; and Charlie Collins' suggestion in *Threads* No. 39 (p. 22) to use dowels for custom knitting needles.
—*Therese M. Inverso, Camden, NJ*

STITCH MARKERS FOR KNITTING

I like to mark my knitting by slipping a bobby pin over certain stitches. I use a black bobby pin for each increase and a silver one for decrease stitches. You could also use a spot of fingernail polish on the bobby pin to indicate whatever you have trouble remembering.

—*Jean Scheffler, Shelbyville, IN*

TWO-ROW KNITTING MARKER

I have found the hybrid marker shown in Fig. 77 to be helpful in circular knitting where shaping is done on alternate rounds (like a raglan sweater knit from the neck down). Instead of trying to remember which kind of row I'm on, I use two colors of marker rings. I slit one with a craft knife and slip it into the other, then pick up the free ring on every round. For me, red means "stop and increase," and green means "go on knitting," but the color isn't important as long as you remember which is which. Yarn loops would work as well.

—*Lisa Mannery, Seattle, WA*

FIG. 77

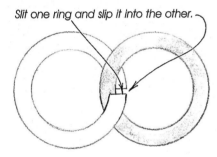

Slit one ring and slip it into the other.

YARN MARKERS

Use scraps of yarn (about 5 in. long) as markers in your knitting—within the row to mark pattern changes, like the beginning of cables, or at the edges of the row to mark increases, etc. Lay the yarn along the completed stitch and knit over it.

I'm knitting a garment whose instructions read, "*Increase every 4th row twice, every 6th row once*. Repeat between *'s 5 times." This means increasing in every 4th row 10 times, and in every 6th row 5 times. I cut 10 lengths of one color to mark every 4th-row increase and 5 lengths of another color to mark the 6th-row increases. When I come back to my work, I can see immediately what I've done last—no need for notes. When the yarn markers are all used, my increase sequence is complete—no need to count or keep track.

Yarn markers are flexible, stay where they're put, are easily removed with a pull, and are free. Avoid strongly contrasting markers with lots of fuzzies—they'll leave telltale fibers.

—*Elizabeth Rothman, Seattle, WA*

I read the "Yarn markers" tip with interest, but I have an easier way to mark knitting or crochet rows. Use plastic closures or ties from bread or produce bags. It's an inexpensive, surefire way to mark increases, decreases, or changes in the pat-

tern. These closures clip on and off easily and won't pull or snag the yarn. I keep mine in a zip-top plastic bag and use them over and over.
—*Sue Fruth, Clearwater, MN*

COUNTING STITCHES

When you have a lot of stitches on your knitting that you will need to count, weave a contrasting yarn in every 10 stitches as you knit the row before. That way, if you have to stop, it's easier to resume counting just a few stitches (fewer than 10) than to start all over.
—*Josette Kilmer, Rancho Palos Verdes, CA*

KNITTING ROW COUNTER

I like to use the barrel-type row counter, but it leaves a large gap when knitting in the round. I solved this problem by putting a bead chain (like a key chain) through the counter and slipping the chain over the needle. Now every time I come to the chain, I turn the numbers one notch.
—*Susan Terry, Orlando, FL*

CABLES IN THE ROUND

When I make an Aran sweater in the round, I use 3- to 4-in. pieces of a contrasting color yarn to mark the turning rows. I simply hang the yarn between two stitches just before turning a cable. The piece of yarn stays put but out of my way and lets me count how many rows I have done between turns.
—*Josette M. Kilmer, Rancho Palos Verdes, CA*

KNITTERS' MEASURING AID

To avoid constant measuring when I knit, I mark the work with a length of thin, non-stretchy yarn, like pearl cotton, a few inches longer than the distance to be knitted. I tie an overhand knot at one end, leaving a loop that fits around the needle, and connect the other end to the knitting, as shown in Fig. 78. I adjust the distance between the two connections to the length of knitting required. When the slack is gone, I've knitted far enough.
—*Ninon deZara/Ronn, Roxbury, CT*

FIG. 78

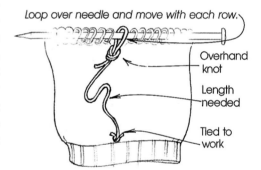

Loop over needle and move with each row.

Overhand knot

Length needed

Tied to work

COMPACT STITCH INSTRUCTIONS

I find it convenient to carry my crochet or knitting instructions written on 3x5 index cards. First I reinforce the edge of the card with tape, and punch a hole next to the instructions for each row or round. I put a safety pin in the hole by the row I am working as a marker. When I need to pack up and go, I attach the safety pin and pattern to the loop of the stitch I am working.
—Anna-Lisa Kanick, Tacoma, WA

FOLLOWING A DIFFICULT PATTERN

I have two ways of keeping track of rows in a difficult knitting pattern. I write each row on a 3x5 index card and flip the cards as I complete each row, or I put my instructions on a metal board with magnetic strips (the kind used for cross-stitch) and position the strip under the row I'm knitting.
—Lynn Teichman, Lewisburg, PA

LISTEN TO YOUR KNITTING PATTERN

Knitting an intricate pattern, such as a lace that requires frequent references to a printed page, can become tiresome after a while. Record the pattern on an audio cassette and replay it as you knit. You're less likely to lose your concentration and your place in the row.
—Sara Tayloe, Arvada, CO

A WAY TO KEEP TRACK OF YOUR KNITTING PATTERN

I like to knit lace, but I used to find it most difficult to keep track of rows or rounds until I saw a person clicking off people going through a gate. I went right out and found my own "people clicker."
—Mary Haverlandt, San Diego, CA

MARKING A PATTERN

I recently used a note from a Scotch Brand Post-it Note Pad to mark the rows on my knitting chart. Placed either above or below the line I was on, it was easy to see and move. I liked it even better than my magnet strips.
—Mary Bright, Cuyohoga Falls, OH

EASY-TO-READ FAIR ISLE KNITTING CHARTS

Keeping your place while knitting Fair Isle can be a chore. Consider those complex predesigned charts where each color is represented by a different symbol. All those symbols jumble together in small squares. How do you sort out the repeats and what the designs look like, and how do you keep your place?

I enlarge the pattern on a copy machine. If it's long, I divide it in half and put it on two sheets of paper. For easy viewing, I divide the pattern evenly into groups of about eight to ten stitches each with colored vertical lines. For a row guide, I cut a piece of 1 in.-wide tacky paper tape or Post-It Correction Tape equal to the width of the pattern, drawing colored lines through the tape to match the pattern. The tape can be moved up the rows easily but will stay put above the row being worked on. For needle markers as I knit, I use loops of embroidery floss that correspond to the vertical color lines drawn on the graph. If I'm knitting a large-size sweater on circular needles, I use many colored markers. But at a glance, I can still tell where I am in my knitting.
—*Helen T. Healy, Lincoln, MA*

I found I was spending a lot of time checking which color went with which letter or symbol on my black and white knitting charts. Now I start my project by coloring the diagram with colored pencils, so I can see at a glance when to change colors.
—*Ethel Roberts, Berkeley, CA*

Using graph paper and crayons, I make my own knitting chart, which is easier to read then published charts. I number the rows, and include my own color key and any helpful notes. To keep my place, I put the chart in a plastic page protector with a cardboard guide clipped to the chart, which I then move up the outside of the chart as I complete each row.
—*Evelyn B. Coyne, Wickliffe, OH*

CUSTOMIZED KNITTING GUIDE SHEETS

When I've designed a sweater using stitch patterns and ideas assembled from various sources and want an easy-to-carry guide, I gather all my reference materials and head for the copy shop where I photocopy each element I need for the garment: gauge, a schematic drawing of the garment, charts, directions, and photos of stitches, and any notes, reducing them if necessary so they'll all fit on a single sheet of paper. Then I assemble all the parts, paste them up, and copy the whole thing. Uncomplicated designs can usually fit on one side of regular or legal-size paper, making a handy permanent record.
—*Jean Margolis, Sebastopol, CA*

KNITTER'S GADGET ORGANIZER

I use a dental organizer to hold my small knitting gadgets (see Fig. 80). This plastic case easily fits into a purse and is at least child-deterring. I bought it at the local drugstore for under $2. It comes in some wonderfully bright colors.

—*Pamela Staveley, Bena, VA*

FIG. 80

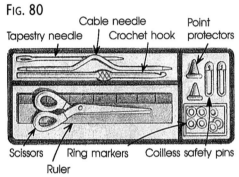

Tapestry needle · Cable needle · Crochet hook · Point protectors

Scissors · Ring markers · Coilless safety pins · Ruler

Use a dental organizer to carry your knitting gadgets neatly and safely.

KEEPING TRACK OF KNITTING

I usually design my own knit or crochet project, so I don't need complete directions for shaping, finishing off, etc., but often I want to keep a record of a particular stitch to use in the future. I type out the directions on a 4-in. by 6-in. index card, then make up a swatch showing one or two repeats (about 2 in. by 3 in.). I staple the swatch to the back of the card to jog my memory.

—*Olive Crook, Green Bay, WI*

KNITTING IN CLOSE QUARTERS

If you're going to be knitting while traveling, especially on an airplane or a bus, it's much easier to knit on circular needles than on straight ones. They take up less elbow room and less space in your bag. You don't need a pattern designed for circular needles, just knit back and forth in the usual way, as if you had two separate needles.

—*Ruth S. Galpin, Southport, CT*

KNITTING TOOLS POUCH

I regularly knit while taking public transportation to and from work and often lose things in my knitting bag. I solved my problem by putting all my equipment, except for the yarn and needles—a 6-in. ruler, a crochet hook for dropped stitches, folding scissors, stitch markers, cable needles, and needle guards—into a sandwich-size zip-top plastic bag. Now I can always find what I need, and I can easily replace the bag when it tears or becomes soiled.

—*Joan M. Harris, Pullman, WA*

KEEP IT CLEAN

When I crochet, knit, or work on my minia-tures, I work off a tray table covered with a large, soft, thin "country cotton" towel. When I lay my work down, I cover it with the ends of the clean towel, and it stays put, despite our eight cats.

—*Nancy Kelly, Brooksville, FL*

EASY-TO-FIND CABLE NEEDLE

To prevent losing my small U-shaped cable needle when it's not in use, I anchor it in the sweater by securing its short end with a point protector.

—*Linda Van Houten, Juneau, AK*

POINT PROTECTORS FOR FOUR-NEEDLE KNITTING

After trying many ways of securing four-needle sets when making socks and mittens, I finally solved the problem by buying point protectors for large needles. The packet I bought held two extra-large flexible point protectors for 4- to 7-mm needles (approx. U.S. sizes 5 to 10½ or English sizes 8 to 2). Each protector will fit over the ends of four small needles, ranging from about 2½ to 3¼ mm (U.S. sizes 1 to 3 or English sizes 13 to 10).

—*L. Manton, Montreal, PQ, Canada*

CABLE HOLDERS

I always use a safety pin to twist the cables in knitting. It is small enough not to get in the way and can be parked and retrieved easily in the work without even unwinding yarn from my fin-gers. At the end of the row I pin it into the bot-tom of the knitting so it's never lost.

—*Margaret Horton, Atlanta, GA*

It's so easy to lose a double-pointed cable knit-ting needle. After trying several alternatives, in-cluding toothpicks, I bought a package of plastic hair-roller picks (the pins used with brush rollers—see Fig. 81). The small knob on one end keeps the pick from sliding through the knitting, where I park it. This knob also secures cabled stitches on the needle, as long as the point is placed downward. The knob is small enough that the stitches can be pulled over it after they have been knitted.

—*Carol L. Douglas, Phoenix, AZ*

FIG. 81

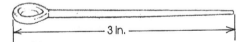

3 In.

EASY-TO-FIND NEEDLE PROTECTORS

To keep from losing my knitting needle protectors, I connect them with a length of yarn stitched through the rubber tips and knotted at the ends. Use a stout needle and leave just enough yarn between the tips so you can use them normally. When the protectors fail, they don't go far. Besides, a pair is easier to find.

—Betty Isaacson, Vancouver, WA

DETACHABLE NEEDLE TIPS FOR TIGHT KNITTING

Tight knitting can make fancy bobble stitches (K3 in a single stitch) difficult to knit because the stitch on the left needle needs to be loose to execute the stitch easily. The use of circular needles with detachable, replaceable tips, found in Boyle needle sets, can solve the problem if you use two different needle tip sizes. Attach a tip the correct gauge to the right-hand needle and a tip two or three sizes smaller to the left-hand needle. The smaller tip makes it possible to knit several stitches together and still knit the finished bobble or other multiple stitch onto the gauge needle without difficulty. Straight-needle knitters can use this trick too by sliding the work onto a smaller needle to knit a bobble, but knitting it onto the needle size needed to obtain gauge.

—Josephine W. Boyd, Fort Collins, CO

CUSTOM KNITTING NEEDLES

I have an easy way to make my own knitting needles in any length I need from white birch dowels. As Fig. 82 shows, standard dowel sizes don't correspond to every needle size, but I find these sizes useful.

Cut the dowels to the length you desire (I use anything from 6 in. to 36 in.), and sharpen one end in a pencil sharpener or with a knife. Sand the needle, especially the end, to remove burrs and smooth the wood. It's important to do a very thorough job of this. Rub the sanded needles with paraffin wax, which will make the yarn slide nicely for easier knitting. To keep the yarn on the needles, I suggest either wrapping a rubber band around the blunt end several times or gluing on a button.

—Charlie Collins, Virgin, UT

FIG. 82

Equivalent needle size		
Dowel diameter (in.)	U.S.	Metric
⅛	3	3.25
³⁄₁₆	6	4
¼	10½	6.5
⁵⁄₁₆	11	7
⅜	13	8

CIRCULAR-NEEDLE STORAGE

Commercial organizers for circular knitting needles just don't suit me. Instead, I store needles in clear plastic sheet protectors from my stationery store (see Fig. 83). The sheets are closed on three sides and open at the top. They have a strip on the side with holes for placing in a binder. Once I label the envelope with the needle size and slide my circular needles inside, I have permanent, see-through storage for my collection.

—*Peg Boren, McAllen, TX*

A CIRCULAR NEEDLE FILE

I use an accordion file folder with multiple pockets (9½ in. by 7½ in., found in office-supply stores) to hold my circular needles and keep them organized. The pockets can be labeled, and each will hold all the lengths of a single size, plus small double-pointed needles. It even has an attached elastic band to keep everything secure just in case it overturns.

—*Beth La Breche, Fridley, MN*

FIG. 83

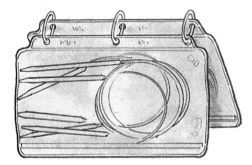

CIRCULAR-NEEDLE HOLDER

I made my own storage holder for circular needles from a 2-in. by 1-yd. strip of notched cardboard folded in half (see Fig. 84). Rubber bands around the notches hold the layers together. My needles slip easily between the layers of the compartments, which I've numbered with the needles' sizes. I made two holders—one for short needles and one for long ones—which hang on separate hangers in my sewing room closet.

—*Eve Sobery, Florissant, MO*

FIG. 84

FIG. 85

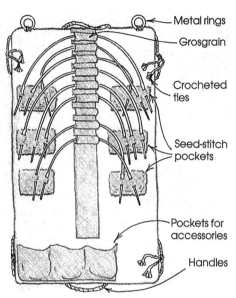

Metal rings
Grosgrain
Crocheted ties
Seed-stitch pockets
Pockets for accessories
Handles

PORTABLE CIRCULAR-NEEDLE STORAGE

Here's how to make an inexpensive portable circular-needle holder: Start with two 17-by-28-in. rectangles of denim (any heavyweight fabric will do). Quilt the back panel to pad the holder. Sew a 2-yd.-long, 24-in.-wide strip of grosgrain ribbon into loops down the center of the front panel. Use your needles as a guide for the loop sizes, and a zipper foot to sew close to them (see Fig. 85). Knit rectangular seed-stitch pockets to punch the points through, and stitch the pockets to the front panel. Add three small pockets on the bottom to hold accessories. My panels were sewn wrong sides together (you can also bind the panels together on the edges). Add crocheted ties to secure the sides when the holder is folded in half, and attach two metal rings at the top to hang it up.

—*Jean W. Jeppson, Midvale, UT*

STORING CIRCULAR NEEDLES

Zip-top plastic bags are ideal for storing circular knitting needles, one per bag. The bags come in various sizes to accommodate the different needle lengths. I put self-adhesive labels on the bags to show the needle sizes and the lengths, and then I file the needles in numerical order for quick retrieval.

—*Sara Tayloe, Arvada, CO*

With a standard three-hole loose-leaf binder and 1-gallon (10⁹⁄₁₆-by-8½-in.) resealable plastic bags you can make a great organizer for a collection of circular needles, or anything else that'll fit into the bags. Reinforce the bottom of the bags by folding them over twice and machine stitching the fold with a long stitch and a size 14 needle (I marked each bag at 8½ in. from the opening and folded to the line to make them all the size I wanted). With an ordinary hole punch, make holes through the folded layers, and label each bag with a permanent marker or by slipping paper labels into them. Each bag will hold several different lengths of the same size needles.

—*Sandee Jaastad, Denver, CO*

MARKERS FOR CIRCULAR NEEDLES

Are your circular knitting needles in a jumble? Mine were. Now, to tell at a glance which needle is what size, I slip one of those plastic bread-closure clips on each needle. I print the needle's size and length on the back of the clip in large letters with a waterproof pen.

—*Kathleen C. Saxe, Sioux City, IA*

RELAXATION TIP

A soak in hot water loosens up a coiled circular knitting needle.

—*Beth Kollé, Seattle, WA*

PHOTOCOPYING TEXTILES

Photocopies of lace, knitting, crochet, macrame, and other textiles are beautiful, easy to make, and have many uses. You can run off multiple copies of a motif in a wink and use them to create new designs that can themselves be copied for further experimentation. Photocopies are excellent to record your own or borrowed work, analyze stitches, reckon gauge, or share ideas. For classes, nothing compares with instructions accompanied by a life-sized photocopy of the project. Copies of your work on good paper are impressive to include with show applications and queries to publishers and to hand out as brochures and samples for customers. These ideas are just the tip of a promising iceberg.

When placed on the copier window, light-colored yarns need a black background, so cover the piece with black cloth, construction paper, or mat board big enough to cover the window. Play with the light-dark settings. If you can find a copier that reduces and enlarges, the possibilities are endless.

—*Ruby Moore, Tallahassee, FL*

SELF-INDEXING

I subscribe to several different knitting-related magazines and was getting tired of flipping through so many back issues looking for that special "idea" I'd once read about. So I created a personal index using a rolodex card file. When a new issue comes in with something I want to remember, I write out a card and file it alphabetically according to topic. I note the magazine, date, and pages. This little extra effort has really saved time and frustration.

—*Marydee Sklar, Portland, OR*

DOCUMENT YOUR WORK

Always take photographs of your finished projects. In time you will have an album full of accomplishments to look back on, and a handy reference when duplicating a past project.

—*Karen McCormic, Many, LA*

Chapter 6

MACHINE KNITTING

Casting on

Machine knitters often cast on with a few rows of waste yarn and then switch to knitting with the fashion yarn, if they plan to pick up the open stitches of the fashion yarn later and machine- or hand-knit a ribbing or other edging. The waste yarn is removed in the finishing process. It holds the stitches until they're needed, at which time you clip and pull out the last row of waste yarn. The rest of the waste yarn falls off, leaving stitches ready for picking up and knitting (see Fig. 86).

Use a smooth, strong yarn that is finer than the fashion yarn, which makes it easier to remove. Leftover cones of 5/2 pearl cotton are appropriate; even fine, strong cotton string on cones (sometimes available in hardware stores) can serve as a wonderful, inexpensive waste yarn. Waste yarn doesn't have to be on cones. Leftover balls of yarn can also be used, although they tend to be smaller and require more frequent replacing than cones, and they tend to tangle more easily.

FIG. 86

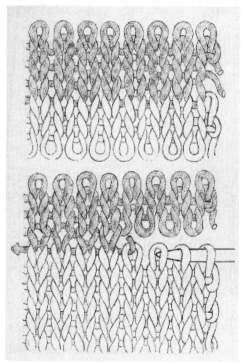

Using the waste yarn

As a new machine knitter, I've been bothered by the tangled waste yarn pulled from each garment. Now I cut a 3-in. by 4-in. bobbin from a piece of cereal-box cardboard, put a small slit at one end to hold the end of the yarn, and wind the waste yarn onto it. I save the cards of waste yarn for plastic canvas stitchery.
—*Audrey Krier, Pine Island, MN*

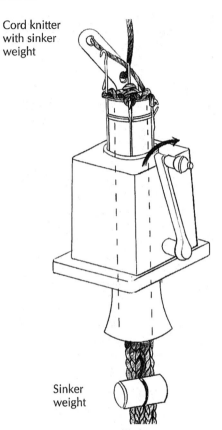

FIG. 87

Cord knitter
with sinker
weight

Sinker
weight

SINKERS

A sinker is a weight used on knitting machines and cord knitters to anchor the knitting and keep enough tension on the yarn so the stitches will form correctly, as shown in Fig. 87. Sinkers are sold as accessories with many knitting machines, but if you need additional weight, such as for working with bulky yarns that tend to catch on the cord knitter, you can use almost anything to weight down the yarn. For example, an opened paper clip or metal hook attached on one end to the yarn and on the other to a sewing weight (for cutting out patterns), a kitchen implement, or a fishing weight (available in sporting goods stores in various sizes) makes a perfectly good yarn weight. The key is to add enough weight for the stitches to knit off smoothly, but not so much weight that it prevents the machine from operating freely.

STRIPED KNITS AND THE NEEDLEMASTER

I've found a strategy to produce honeycomb shapes for my scrap afghan. To make equilateral hexagons, I cast on 12 sts and increase as per the pattern. When the stitches on the needle equal three times the number cast on (36), I decrease until I reach the number cast on. Then I bind off.

Also, using the Boye NeedleMaster kit, I've found that when the coupler starts to wear, I can make a fresh start by snipping the ⅛ in. of worn plastic from each end. The loss in length will hardly be noticeable during the next several jaunts around the world with this versatile kit.
—*Thomas Walsh, Seattle, WA*

USE IT UP

I use the tension swatch yarn from machine knitting for hand work like weaving seams, crocheting necklines, and sleeve edgings. I can take my knitting project with me to finish on vacation without taking extra yarn along.
—*Sharon Collins, Pocatello, ID*

PRECISE CUT-AND-SEW NECKLINES FOR MACHINE KNITTERS

Although I prefer to machine knit fabric to shape, it is sometimes necessary or easier to use the cut-and-sew method at the neckline. This is especially true of double jacquard, many double-bed fabrics, and some patterning stitches such as tuck, slip, or a complex Fair Isle. I have discovered two methods of marking the seamline while knitting that ensure the neckline is cut precisely. I use these methods with an automatic patterning device, but they could also be used with a written pattern.

For double-jacquard fabrics, knit the pattern until the neckline shaping begins. Following the drawn or written pattern, transfer the stitches indicated for binding off from the ribber bed to the main bed. Place the ribber needles into nonworking position following the transfer. Continue knitting in pattern to the top of the garment, transferring stitches as necessary. It may be necessary to pull those needles holding transferred stitches to upper working or holding position before knitting every row so that they knit every time. The area transferred to the main bed knits in tiny stripes with stitches much smaller than the rest of the pattern, making it easy to see where the neckline is to be cut, as shown in the top drawing of Fig. 88. Cut about ¼ in. above the regular jacquard pattern.

Fig. 88

Double-jacquard fabric

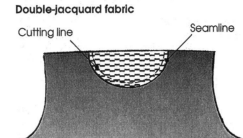

Cutting line   Seamline

Single-bed fabric

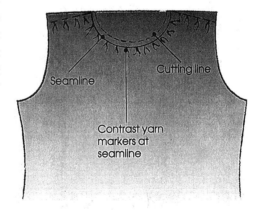

Seamline

Cutting line

Contrast yarn markers at seamline

The tiny stitches in the cut area hold together tightly, and there is little danger of unraveling with careful handling.

For other double-bed fabrics, the area being transferred becomes a single-bed fabric easily distinguishable from the main pattern. As a single-bed fabric, it is also more stable when being cut.

For single-bed fabrics, when neckline shaping is reached, lay short lengths of contrast yarn in the hooks of selected needles to mark the stitches that would normally be bound off. For the first bind-off, which may involve 10 to 20 stitches, mark the first, middle, and last stitches with the contrast yarn and, holding onto the contrast yarn as the carriage passes it, knit the row. Be careful not to pull the needles out of position when laying in the contrast yarn; doing so will cause the pattern to knit incorrectly. Continue knitting in pattern, marking the line of shaping every four to six rows. This will give a precise line to follow when cutting (see the bottom drawing of Fig. 88). Cut ¼ in. above the line. I leave the yarn markers attached while positioning the garment and neckband on the machine for linking together.

—*Peggy C. Durant, Clearfield, PA*

FULLY FASHIONED DECREASES AND INCREASES

Fully fashioned decreases create a smooth selvage. Move a stitch or group of stitches from the edge toward the center of the work, so that the needle at the point of decrease carries two stitches. Use a transfer tool to shift all the

FIG. 89

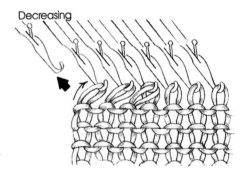

Decreasing

Increasing

90

stitches outside the decrease at once, if possible (see Fig. 89).

Increases are similar, but to prevent a hole, lift a bar from the row below to fill the empty needle.

SMOCKING ON MACHINE KNITS

I recently decided to use smocking to control the stretching I anticipated in a ribbed, drop-shoulder sweater I was machine-knitting. I set the tension tighter at each row I planned to smock so it was easy to see horizontal lines. The smocking went quickly, and the shoulders didn't sag.
—*D. Bird, Guemes Island, WA*

MANAGING YARN ENDS ON THE KNITTING MACHINE

When introducing a new yarn at the end of a machine-knit row, instead of attaching the end to the stand after threading the carriage, take the end from under the carriage and manually knit the first stitch with it. Snip the new and old ends to 2 in. or 3 in., and clip them together with a clothespin so they hang from the work and weight the new stitch. This saves yarn, the work is neater and you don't have to remember to untie the ends from the stand later.
—*Enid Zucker, Southbury, CT*

TUCKS

To machine knit a tuck, work twice as many rows as the desired width of the tuck in whatever pattern you desire. Use a one-, two-, or three-prong transfer tool to hang the last row of loops of the background yarn over the stitches on the final row of the tuck, as shown in Fig. 90. This will fold the tuck rows in half and cause a raised tuck to form on the right side of the work. Raise the tension one or two numbers to knit the next row in the background yarn. Then resume normal knitting tension.

FIG. 90

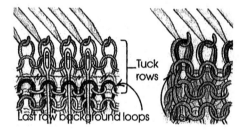

Tuck rows

Last row background loops

MACHINE-KNITTING WITH NO LOOSE ENDS

When I'm machine-knitting a design that requires color changing, I get rid of the cut ends by looping, or E-wrapping, them around several needles on the next two or three rows. This locks in the ends, which don't show on the right side and which can be clipped away.
—*Barbara Flett, Princeton, BC, Canada*

ISOLATION LACE

I have a Genie kh-710 Brother knitting machine that has a lace carriage but no isolation capabilities. Here's how I make isolation lace motifs anyway.

I knit the garment in stockinette but don't assemble it. Then I shape and knit the lace pattern with my lace carriage. Using a fade-away fabric marker, I trace the design on the garment where I want it. If I think that extra support or a backing is necessary, I put a piece of nylon organdy on top of the outline. Using a serger or a zigzag stitch on my sewing machine, I sew around the tracing, covering the edges of the nylon organdy. Then I turn the piece over and carefully cut away only the stockinette stitches inside the stitching.

Finally, with the garment right side up, I pin the lace design in place over the cutout or cutout and organdy, being sure to cover the serging stitches. When I use a straight stitch and sewing machine to attach the lace, I also edge it with purchased lace. For a completely knit look, I duplicate-stitch by hand around the lace, using the same yarn.

—*Ellen J. Riggan, Gloucester, VA*

AN ALTERNATIVE TO TUBULAR BIND-OFF

I do most of my knitting on a standard-gauge knitting machine and work the ribbing by hand from the top down when the pieces are complete, using small (0 to 2) needles. It's hard to get a good tubular cast-off in a small gauge, but I've found that a technique of Elizabeth Zimmermann's gives a neat, elastic edge.

Hold the work on a single needle with the right side facing you. Break off the yarn, leaving a tail about four times the length of the piece to be bound off, and thread it on a tapestry needle. Bring the needle through the second loop from the end from right to left and back to front. Then insert the needle into the first stitch from left to right and front to back, and slip the flint stitch off the needle, as shown in Fig. 91.

FIG. 91

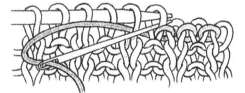

Insert tapestry needle from right to left and back to front in second stitch from point of knitting needle. Then go left to right and front to back in end stitch, and drop it.

92

Repeat across with an even tension. When you get to the last pair of stitches, bring the needle through the top of the first stitch to the back of the work, and weave it in.

—*Patricia Tongue Edraos, Boston MA*

FIXING PUNCH-CARD ERRORS

When punching new patterns for the knitting machine, I often make a mistake or decide to change a design after sampling. To cover a space that I punch incorrectly, I use white freezer tape. It's much better than clear tape because it gives the visual aid I need in punching.

—*Hannelore Ring, San Diego, CA*

KNIT YOUR OWN COIL

You can make your own coil or rope with a knitting machine. Double-bed knitting machines can be set to knit circular tubes of various sizes, by placing one of the beds out of work. If your machine is a single bed, you will have to move the cam box back to the right side after knitting the stitches right to left. Pass the yarn under the needles before beginning your next row of stitches. Knit the rope using a tight tension and a firm yarn. This knitted coil can be used to make baskets, rugs, or mats either by hand or sewing machine. The coil needs no core or fabric scraps.

—*Ellen Riggan, Gloucester, VA*

DRAWING KNITTING-MACHINE PATTERNS

To draw accurate half-scale patterns for my knitting machine, I use a Macintosh computer and MacDraft (Innovative Data Design Inc., 2280 Bates Ave., Suite A, Concord, CA 94520; 415-680-6818). This software is used primarily for architectural drawing. With it you can draw smooth arcs for a neckline and can print to quarter and half scales.

After drawing the garment pattern, you can add original intarsia designs, place a single decorative motif wherever you like, etc. These design elements can be easily manipulated without disrupting the garment pattern, which can be reprinted with or without them.

—*Mary Louise Vidas, Mount Airy, NC*

Chapter 7

CROCHET

GETTING STARTED

A slip knot and chain is the basis of all crochet. Make a slip knot by forming a loop and pulling the yarn from behind the loop through to the front with the crochet hook, as shown in the left-hand drawings of Fig. 92; tighten gently. Make a chain by wrapping the yarn over the hook (yo), and pulling the hook and yarn through the loop, as shown in the right-hand drawing of Fig. 92; tighten and repeat.

FIG. 92

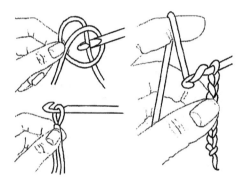

CROCHET COUNTING AIDS

I usually crochet with a tray table in front of me, and I count rows or stitches by moving whatever is on the table—pencils, paper clips, spoons, a coffee cup. I build a pile and then "unbuild" the pile. Moving a small item is faster than picking up a pen and writing after each row.

—*Nancy Kelly, Brooksville, FL*

SINGLE CROCHET

Single crochet (sc) is a two-step stitch that's relatively short in height and is useful for fitting a lot of detailed patterning into a small area; it makes a firm, nonstretchy fabric. Insert the hook from front to back through both loops of the stitch below (see Fig. 93). Yo and pull up a loop; you now have two loops on the hook. Yo again, and pull through both loops.

FIG. 93

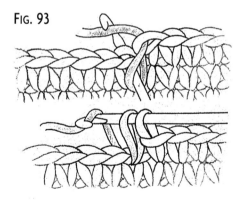

FIG. 94

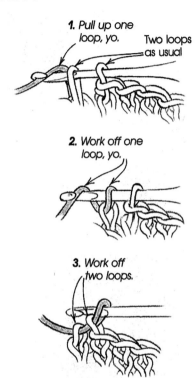

1. Pull up one
loop, yo.
Two loops
as usual

2. Work off one
loop, yo.

3. Work off
two loops.

SQUARE SINGLE CROCHET

Single crochet isn't a square stitch, which causes a problem in following graphed or charted designs. To make a square single crochet, put the hook through the completed row as usual, yo, and pull up a loop (two loops on the hook). Yo; work off one loop, leaving two loops on the hook; then yo and work off both loops (see Fig. 94). This really puts a chain stitch in the middle, adding just enough extra height to square the stitch.

—*Edith Frankel, Hannawa Falls, NY*

DOUBLE CROCHET

Double crochet (dc) results in a taller stitch that works up more quickly than sc. Yo, insert the hook through the loops as for sc, then yo and pull up a loop; you now have three loops on the hook, as shown in Fig. 95. Yo and pull through two of the loops, then yo again and pull through the remaining two loops on the hook.

FIG. 95

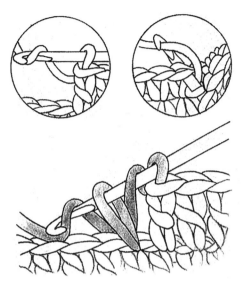

INCREASING AND DECREASING

To increase (inc), crochet (sc or dc) two stitches in one stitch, as shown in Fig. 96.

Working a decrease (dec) narrows crochet by eliminating a stitch. To decrease in sc, start by pulling up a loop as usual. Now insert the hook into the following stitch, yo, and pull up a loop (see the top drawing of Fig. 97); yo and pull yarn through all three loops on the hook. To decrease in dc, start by working a stitch as usual; stop at the last step when there are two loops left on the hook. Yo, insert the hook into the following stitch and pull up a loop, yo and pull through two loops, then yo and pull through the remaining three loops on the hook, as shown in the bottom drawing of Fig. 97.

FIG. 97

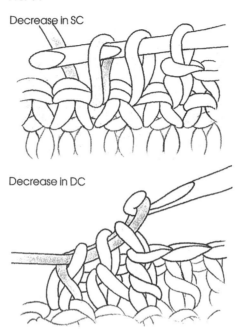

Decrease in SC

Decrease in DC

FIG. 96

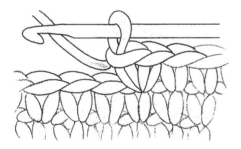

FIG. 103A

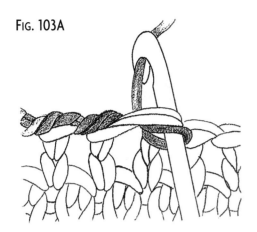

FIG. 103B

CRAB-STITCH CROCHET

Crab-stitch crochet, also called backwards crochet, produces a beautiful corded edging. It's worked almost like single crochet, except from left to right. Work a row of single crochet from right to left, as usual. Do not turn the work. Chain one, *insert the hook under the next stitch to the right, pick up the yarn by dropping the head of the hook over it, and draw up a long loop (see Fig. 103A). Wrap yarn over the hook and pull through both loops on the hook (Fig. 103B).* Repeat from *-*.

CORRECTING UNEVEN CROCHET EDGES

To eliminate the undesirable holes and gaps that sometimes occur at the end of a row of double crochet, a correction is often made in the space after the turning chain. But I was not pleased with this result and discovered that changing the length of the turning chain from three to two stitches reduces the slack. Chain 2 and turn counterclockwise for a cleaner edge.
—*Gladys Shue, York, PA*

WORKING INTO THE FRONT OR BACK LOOP

Crochet is usually worked into both the front and back loops at the top of a stitch in the row below, with the hook inserted from front to back. When you insert the hook in the front loop (front of loop) only or back loop (back of loop) only of the stitch, as shown in Fig. 104, the other loop remains on the fabric as a horizontal bar. This bar becomes part of the pattern or serves as a loop to be picked up and worked later.

FIG. 104

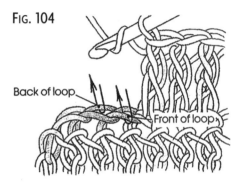

Back of loop

Front of loop

FILET CROCHET

Filet crochet forms designs from square meshes of solid and open crochet. Each open mesh is made of three chain stitches separated by one double crochet, and four double crochets make the solid blocks. Directions for filet crochet are often given in charts similar to knitting charts. To read the chart (see Fig. 105), right-handers begin in the bottom right-hand corner and read row 1 to the left, then row 2 to the right. Open squares in the chart represent meshes, while dots indicate solid blocks.

FIG. 105

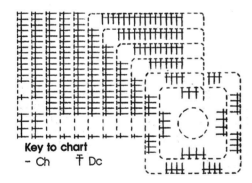

Key to chart
- Ch   ⊤ Dc

PERFECT CROCHET JOINERY

Are you bothered by the not-so-perfect join at the beginning and end of a decorative, finishing round of single crochet? Try this invisible join: Begin the round by inserting the hook in the spot desired and pull a loop through. Do not chain, but work a single crochet in the next stitch and all around the piece. When you return to the beginning, work the last stitch loop as usual. Cut the yarn. Complete the last stitch by pulling the end through the two loops on the hook (see Fig. 106). Take a tapestry needle and thread the yarn end under the original beginning loop and back in the top of the last chain where the single crochet stitches ended. This new chain completes the first stitch of the round.

—*Susan Z. Douglas, Topsham, ME*

FIG. 106

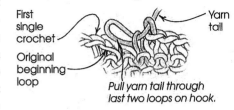

First single crochet

Original beginning loop

Yarn tail

Pull yarn tail through last two loops on hook.

Thread tail under beginning loop and into last chain stitch.

Finish the "V" on the back and weave the tails into the work.

UNTWISTED CROCHET TURNING CHAINS

If you find it difficult to enter your turning chain from the previous crocheted row to pick up a stitch, you may have twisted it in turning your work. To avoid this, always turn the piece away from your body, counterclockwise for right-handers and clockwise for lefties.
—*Gladys Shue, York, PA*

MAKING A ROUND CORD

Here's a quick way to crochet a round and even cord of any length or thickness, using no hook, only your hands.

For a small cord, start with yarn at least six times the length you want the finished cord to be. Fold the yarn in half and make a slip loop. Working with both forefingers, alternately pull the yarn through the loop, first from one side and then from the other (see the top drawing of Fig. 107). Slip the loop alternately from the holding finger to the other forefinger as it makes the new loop, pulling down on the cord as it forms (bottom drawing). You'll find the motion is easy once you get it. When you reach the desired length, pull the loose ends through the loop and weave them into the cord.

For a thick cord, start with multiple strands of yarn—double, triple, etc. There are endless uses for a cord like this—ties for hats, booties,

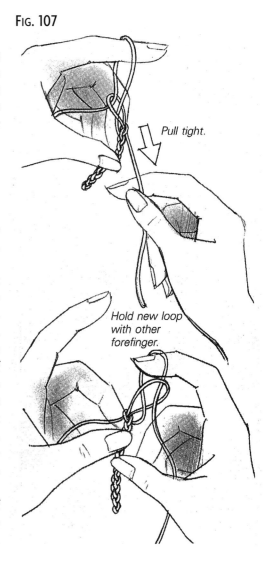

FIG. 107

Pull tight.

Hold new loop with other forefinger.

sweaters, plant hangers, even shoelaces. I've made sneaker laces using two school colors of fine orlon or nylon yarn. A tight wrap of Scotch tape, wax, or glue will shape the tips.

—*Jean Leavitt, Newtown, CT*

CROCHET A WAISTBAND

Here's a great way to crochet a sweater waistband with the "elastic" stretch of a knit. Using a fine yarn or floss that gives about 8 single-crochet (sc) stitches (sts) to the inch, chain (ch) 26 sts with a No. 3 steel crochet hook. Sc in 2nd chain from hook and in each ch across (25 sc). This row of 25 sc is your foundation chain. Ch 1, turn each row. Sc in back loop (lp) of each sc across. Repeat last row until piece, when slightly stretched, measures 30 in. (for sizes 10-12) or desired waist measurement. Don't cut the thread when you finish; you'll use it to join the ends of the waistband to make a circle.

Next row: Slip stitch together (sl st) back lp of first sc (the first sc on the last row of the waistband) and first st of the foundation chain, *sl st together back lp of next sc and next st in chain*, repeat from * across. End off. Sew the waistband to the lower edge of the sweater, easing the sweater to fit.

—*Marilyn J. Panter, Walnut Creek, CA*

AN ALTERNATIVE TO THE PLAIN CHAIN

Here's an attractive, sturdy, and more finished-looking alternative to an ordinary crocheted chain foundation. It's ideal when you won't be adding another edge to the crocheted piece. Start with a slip knot. While holding it loose, make one chain. Insert the hook in the slip knot again and draw the thread through so that there are two loops on the hook, as shown in Fig. 108. Draw the thread through both of them, then adjust the tension to even out the stitch you just made. *Pull slightly to get some slack on the loop on the hook, then insert the hook in the loop closest to the hook. Pull the thread through the two loops now on the hook. Repeat from *. This cord also makes a strong, good-looking button loop or belt loop. Leave a long tail at the beginning and at the end of the cord to sew into the seam allowance of the garment.

—*Gladys Shue, York, PA*

FIG. 108

PAIN-FREE CROCHET

Hours of working with a crochet hook take a toll on my hands and wrists, so I've experimented with padding the hook handles. A bigger grip is helpful, but tape and padding seem to slip off eventually. When my husband changed the gas lines in his car a while back, he had several feet of clear rubber tubing left over, so I tried slipping the tubing over the handle of my crochet hook, and it worked beautifully. The hose slides onto the smaller hooks easily, gripping the handle without slipping. (You'll have to pad the smallest hooks with masking tape first, though.) For larger sizes, dipping the hook into hand lotion makes insertion easier. If the handle still seems too narrow, larger diameter rubber hoses are available. Gas-line hose can be found at any auto parts store and costs less than 50¢/ft. A foot of hose will cover three or four handles with a comfortable, nonslip grip. Best of all, my hands no longer ball into fists while I sleep.
—*Suzanne Deal-Fitzgerald, Monticello, GA*

CROCHET A RUFFLE

To make a ruffle at the cuff of a glove, increase in every other stitch or every stitch in the first row to make the ruffle as full as you want; experiment on a swatch.

CROCHETED EDGINGS ON WOVENS

Attaching crocheted edges to firmly woven materials can be difficult if the yarn is too bulky to be drawn easily through the material. I use cotton embroidery floss to make a row of chain stitches about a seam's width from the edge of the material. I can then attach crocheted strips or shapes by single crocheting them to the chain loops, or I can crochet an edging by working directly from the chained line. When they match the color of the edging, the cotton stitches are virtually invisible.
—*Elizabeth Meineke, Prescott, AZ*

HANDMADE CROCHET HOOKS

FIG. 109

Ten years ago, my husband bought me two handmade wooden crochet hooks for Christmas. Since I was afraid that they'd break or that the fancy decorations on the ends would chip off, I didn't use either one until recently. Besides, I thought that they were too fancy to be functional. I was wrong on all counts. The special features of a handmade wooden hook (see Fig. 109) are the lump in the handle, the beads at the end, and the style of the taper. The lump and the beads are both handy when you want to put your work down for a while. If you poke the wooden hook through the fabric in two places with the lump in the middle, the hook stays put. Slide the working loop onto the bead section near the end of the hook. Tighten it, and it will stay there.

I thought that the absence of a thumb rest would be a problem in controlling tension. It would be for fine thread, but for worsted or sport-weight wool, it doesn't make a difference. I also thought that the variable taper would cause stitch inconsistencies, but it doesn't.

—*Mary McGoveran, Boulder Creek, CA*

Beads

Lump

Put hook twice through work with lump in middle to hold it; use beads to secure loop.

FIG. 115

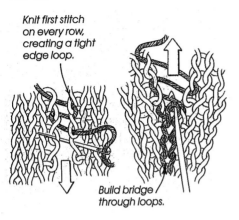

Knit first stitch on every row, creating a tight edge loop.

Build bridge through loops.

VERTICAL KNIT GRAFTING

Have trouble grafting two pieces of knitting vertically? Here's a way to graft two stockinette pieces that makes the seam invisible and, with lighter-weight yarns, cannot be felt: Take a long strand of yarn and, starting at the top of the pieces on the stockinette side, join the edges with yarn lengths equal to that of one dropped stitch (see Fig. 115). (The yarn of one dropped stitch should be about four times the width of one knitted stitch.) When you have done the entire seam, take a crochet hook with a shank the same diameter as your knitting needle and, working from bottom to top, start picking up that "dropped" stitch. The last stitch on your hook will have to be woven in or fastened off.
—*Betty Salpekar, Pittsford, NY*

JOINING RIBBING

After several years of seeking the perfect rib, I have developed various techniques for joining ribbing. One of my favorites is varying the selvages. For a 1x1 rib, put two knit stitches on each edge of the front, the back, and the cuffs. Mattress-stitch into the center of the second stitch from each edge. The result is what looks like a knit stitch at the join. The extra half-knit stitch on the seam rolls down slightly and produces a neater seam than you would get by grafting a knit stitch to a purl stitch, where the knit stitch always seems to roll over onto the purl stitch.

For a 2x2 rib, edge both sides of one piece with two knit stitches, and edge both sides of the other piece with three knit stitches. Or put two knit stitches on one edge and three knit stitches on the other edge of each piece, making sure that you will be joining a three-stitch edge to a two-stitch edge. Again, mattress-stitch through the center of the second stitch from each edge.

The best joining method of all is totally invisible because there is no join. Even when you knit a sweater in separate, flat pieces, you can make a perfect ribbing by knitting it on circular needles after you join the side seams of the sweater with mattress stitch. Begin the pieces above the rib with an invisible cast-on. After you have assembled the garment, pick up the bottom stitches on a circular needle, making sure that you catch each selvage stitch after the second stitch from the edge. When you come around to the selvage stitch on each side, knit or purl it together with the stitch next to, and overlapping, it. You can do cuffs the same way with double-pointed needles.
—*Patricia Tongue Edraos, Boston, MA*

SEAMING WITH SLIP-STITCH CROCHET

Slip-stitch crochet produces a firm, even seam for joining two pieces of knitting. If possible, use yarn about half the weight of the project yarn in the same color so the seam won't be too bulky and it won't show. Place the pieces right sides together and *insert the hook through both pieces between the selvage or edge stitch and the next stitch, as shown in Fig. 116. Catch the yarn and draw through a loop*. Repeat *-* and draw second loop through first loop; one loop remains. Continue drawing second loop through first loop to end of seam. To keep the seam flexible, be sure not to work too tightly.

FIG. 116

BASEBALL STITCH

Use baseball stitch to sew two pieces of knitting together without a bulky seam. Leave a long cast-on tail on one piece to use for sewing. Thread the yarn onto a blunt tapestry needle and butt the two edges to be joined right sides up. Bring the needle up from the wrong side through the edge loop of the unattached piece, then across to the first piece and up through its next edge loop from its wrong side (see Fig. 117).

BLOCKING MIXED YARN SWEATERS

Combining yarns with different fiber contents produces interesting knitted effects and uses up leftover yarns, but the finished product can be difficult to block. Here's how I smooth the lumps and bumps in a multiyarn sweater: Thoroughly wet a large towel. Wring out the excess water and place the towel on a clean, flat surface (the top of a dryer works well). Carefully block and pin your sweater to half of the wet towel. Fold the other half over the sweater to form a sandwich and leave it for half a day. Uncover the sweater and leave it pinned to the towel overnight. In the morning remove the towel and let your sweater dry flat. All those bumps and lumps should disappear.

—*Veronica Schmerling, Pittsburgh, PA*

FIG. 117

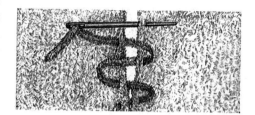

FIG. 118

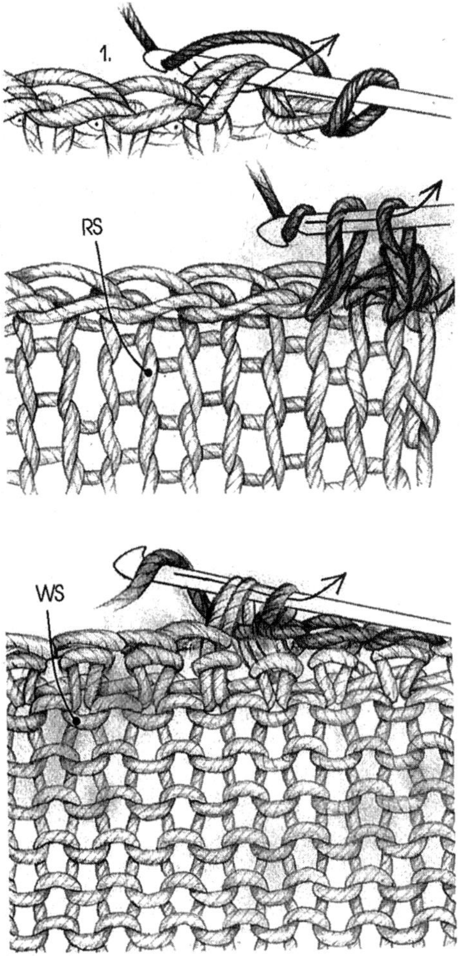

1.

RS

WS

CROCHETED EDGE FINISH

Make a non-rolling finish on your knits using single crochet (sc) and slip stitch on bound-off edges. With the right side of the garment facing you, draw up one loop under the first bind-off chain with a crochet hook, using either matching or contrasting yarn. To make a chain (ch), wrap the yarn over the hook (yo) and pull the yarn through the loop on the hook (step 1). Make one more ch, then draw up one loop through the second bind-off chain (2 loops on hook). Yo, draw through both loops (step 2, 1 sc made).

On the sweater bottom, sc across, ch 1, and turn. Then, from the wrong side, slip-stitch under both loops of each single crochet (see Fig. 118). For circular hems like sleeves, sc around and join last st to 1st sc with a slip stitch. Ch 1, turn, and work the slip stitch from inside the sleeve.

TWO STRAIGHT PINS HOLD KNITTING BEST

If I have to pin baste my knitted garment together while I finish it, I use pairs of straight pins instead of one. Whether they end up parallel or crossed doesn't matter. While one pin may fall out easily, two pins lock each other in place. They do not move, even when I manipulate the knitted pieces.

—*Kristina Deimel, Bearsville, NY*

MACHINE SEWING ON KNITTING

When machine-stitching the armholes of my circular sweaters before cutting the center stitch for the opening, I used to have problems with the yarn catching in the feed dogs. I solved the problem by pinning a used fabric-softener sheet on the wrong side of the sweater, directly below the area to be stitched. The sheet tears away easily after I've stitched down both sides of the armhole.
—Susan Terry, Norfolk, VA

HELPING HANDS WORK INSIDE SMALL KNIT ITEMS

When sewing in the tail ends, stitching a duplicate stitch, or sewing a reinforcement seam in a small, tubular knit item, such as a child's mitten, I find it very helpful to use a darning egg to keep the two layers of fabric separate and to help spread the fabric without overstretching it. The handle of the egg can also slip into a thumb or glove finger quite nicely.
—Ann Prochowicz, Trempealeau, WI

I have recently braved knitting socks for the first time. Although it all went fairly smoothly, I found grafting the toe to be somewhat delicate an operation. To that end, I have found it help-ful to insert a shampoo bottle (any flat-topped container about 2 in. wide would do) into the sock to provide a small table upon which the remaining stitches can be grafted. The bottle itself goes between my knees, thus raising the sock to the perfect height and allowing me to hold it firmly without using my hands.
—Stacey Callahan, Toulouse, France

MAKING DESIGNER LABELS

I use white ⅜-in. satin ribbon and textile paints to make color-coordinated labels for the garments I knit. The paints, nontoxic acrylics, are available at hobby shops in a variety of mixable colors. They come in ready-to-use 1-oz. bottles. I use Badger Air-Tex textile air-brush colors (Badger Air-Brush Co., 9128 W. Belmont Ave., Franklin Park, IL 60131; 708-678-3104).

Paint a length of ribbon, being sure to saturate the fabric. After it has dried, set the colors with an iron. Then, using a fine-point indelible pen, write your labels. The paint works like sizing and prevents the ink from bleeding. Wash out any excess dye. If you prefer white labels, use white paint.
—Mary Louise Vidas, Mount Airy, NC

ADDING FRINGE

Fringe adds an attractive finish at the edges of a rug, and it's an easy detail to do. First, decide on the desired length for the fringe. Wrap yarn around a piece of cardboard cut to that size plus ½ in. for tying; you could also use an object that's the right size, such as a book or box. Cut the yarn along one side of the cardboard to create separate double-length strands. With a crochet hook, pull a group of two to three strands from back to front through the first hole on one end of the rug (as shown in Fig. 119), even the ends, and then tie them in a square knot close to the rug. Repeat for each hole across the width. Trim the ends evenly, if necessary. For a variegated effect, you can combine different colors from the rug to make the fringe.

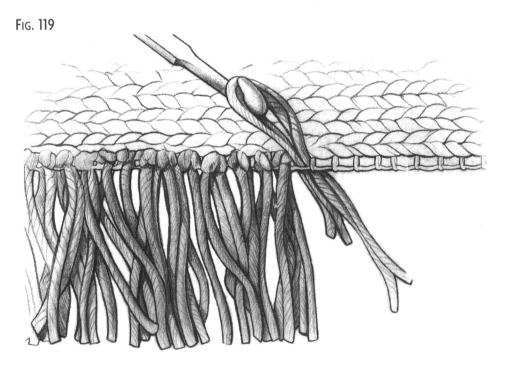

FIG. 119

UNUSUAL SURFACES AID KNITTERS

A wonderful surface for blocking knits is a new carpet remnant that has a canvas backing. Turn it upside down and lay brown paper or cloth over the canvas to make a smooth, clean surface. The canvas is stiff, allows pins to go through easily, and holds the pins in position. The plush carpet fibers on the opposite side hold the canvas off the floor.
—*Susan Terry, Orlando, FL*

Using a small hand-held steamer to fluff knits and flatten seams can be difficult because the steamer needs to be held upright to work properly. Instead, lay your knit garment on an old cork bulletin board and lean the board against a wall. The wool fibers stick to the pebbled surface so the sweater stays in place. This also makes it easy to reposition the sweater to steam all the surface areas.
—*Deborah Newton, Providence, RI*

GROOMING FRINGE

A wide-toothed plastic comb, sometimes called a pick or a hair-lift, works nicely to align all the strands when I'm pressing and trimming the fringe on knitted and crocheted shawls. I have purchased a few combs with different tooth widths for working with a variety of fringes.
—*Lois Manton, Montreal, PQ, Canada*

SIGNING YOUR SWEATERS

Surface embroidery is an elegant and distinctive way to label knitwear or embellish the outside. I sign my sweaters by writing my name on a piece of cross-stitch canvas or organdy, basting this canvas to the finished knit, and then working over my signature in chain stitch, just catching the surface of the knit through the canvas. When the embroidery is done, I trim away the canvas, slipping out the last threads with tweezers. Cotton floss gives a subtle effect, but silk buttonhole twist stands out a bit more. The chain stitch moves easily with the knit fabric.
—*Jane F. Jull, Friday Harbor, WA*

FAIR ISLE SELF-LABELS

Any machine knitter or determined hand knitter can make a label from the yarn used in the garment. A self-label won't scratch; will have the same color, texture, and care as your work; and makes a great impression. It's fabulous on a one-of-a-kind or limited-edition item.

1. Choose two contrasting yarns of the type used in the piece.

2. Separate the yarns into single plies. If you want a raised effect for the letters, you can use a double ply for them.

3. Knit a monogram or trademark in Fair Isle (1½ in. x 1 in.).

4. Hand-sew all four sides of the label loosely to the piece.

5. Attach a fiber-content and care tag to the label, using yarn and a safety pin.
—*Gloria Babiarz, Windsor Locks, CT*

PIZZA-PAN TAM STRETCHERS

A pizza pan from your local housewares store makes a great stretcher for knit tams. The pan is unbreakable, lightweight, and inexpensive, and it comes in many sizes including 12 in. and 14 in.
—*Suzanne Correira, Austin, TX*

NIFTY GIFT TAG

When giving a handknit sweater as a gift, I cut a sweater-shaped tag from cardboard and punch a hole in one shoulder (see Fig. 120). On the tag I write care and cleaning instructions, and fiber content. I wrap a small amount of the sweater's yarn around the middle in case it's needed for mending a hole or seam; then I tie my custom tag to the sweater with a bow.

—*Lynn Teichman, Lewisburg, PA*

FIG. 120

100% wool
Hand wash,
cold. Dry flat.

REPAIRING KNITS

You can repair a single-stitch sweater hole before it becomes a major project. Gently pull the broken end of the yarn out of the torn stitch. Follow the path of the broken end with replacement yarn threaded on a tapestry needle. Do one loop at a time, replacing all the stitches you wish to repair. I use three-ply Persian tapestry wool (found in most yarn stores), which comes in a variety of colors and can be unraveled.

You can also replace a portion of a knitted pattern whose color no longer pleases you with the same technique. No ripping back to the offending color and reknitting.

—*Lynne Vogel, Canyon Beach, OR*

When mending small holes in fine-gauge woolen knitwear, it's not always possible to secure the yarn you are using to the frayed edges of the hole. I felt the join slightly instead of overmending with extra stitches. Turn the sweater inside out after making the repair and lay it on a clean, white towel. Dampen the mended area with a blend of soap and hot water (cautiously proceed with any multicolored garment). Wait until the mixture is thoroughly absorbed into the fibers before rubbing the join gently with a soft toothbrush. This will mat the fibers together.

—*Susan Herrmann, Damascus, OH*

WASHING GREASY WOOL

Washing greasy fleece, such as merino, does not have to be difficult and tedious if you know how. There are only two ingredients in the recipe:

• 2 cups of pure soap flakes, such as Ivory or Lux (if you can't find flakes, shave a bar of pure soap).

• Denatured alcohol (you can get it at a hardware store).

Slowly pour sufficient alcohol into the soap flakes, stirring constantly, until the mixture is a thick, creamy paste. The mixture will keep for years in a screw-top jar.

To wash 5 lb. of greasy wool, put 2 gal. of hot, but not boiling, water into a sink or washtub. You must just be able to keep your hands in the water. Add 2 tbsp. of the creamy mixture and stir until it becomes sudsy. Place the wool in a mesh basket or on a wire screen and dunk it slowly in and out of the water 20 to 30 times. Rinse it in warm, clean water until all the suds are gone. If the wool has any smell, place a small amount of vinegar in the rinse water to remove the odor. Dry the wool on a rack in the sun. Wire netting or a wire platform is ideal.

The wool must dry fairly quickly—within 48 hours—or it could be damaged. The alcohol remains active while it is wet and literally eats up the grease. If the wool remains wet too long, the alcohol may eat the wool fibers as well.

If the wool is exceptionally dirty, you may have to wash it a second time after you've rinsed it. Repeat the process with a new solution. Do not simply add more soap to the dirty water.
—*Cyril Lieschke, Henty, NSW, Australia*

SOFTENING AN ITCHY SWEATER

Sheep's wool is in many ways like human hair. After washing a woolen sweater, I rinse it with vinegar to restore the pH balance. If it's itchy, I soften it with a mixture of 2 tbsp. to 6 tbsp. of hair conditioner and a minimum amount of water, which I spread over the entire garment and between the fibers. After a few minutes, I rinse the sweater thoroughly, towel-dry it, and lay it flat to finish drying.
—*Shelley Karpilow, Berkeley, CA*

WASHING CASHMERE

For years now, I've been washing my wool and cashmere knits in the washing machine. Don't hyperventilate yet. My method simply makes use of the washer's capabilities, assuming you can control some of the functions manually.

Start the washer filling, add your soap or wool detergent, and let mix well. Fold each garment into a neat bundle, as you would when packing for a trip. Distribute these bundles evenly around the washer tub (four is my limit). Let the washer fill until the water level just covers the garments, and turn off the machine. Squish the bundles by hand a bit, then let soak a few minutes. After making sure the items are still in their bundles, set the control to drain the tub and let spin for 10 to 15 seconds. Follow the same procedure for the rinse, allowing the tub to spin just a little longer. Shape and dry flat as usual.

I've never had any stretching or felting using this procedure, and I find it far easier than regular hand washing.
—*Lynn Roosevelt, Greenville, SC*

FLUFFIER HANDSPUN YARN

This process, which I came across in the *New Zealand Woolcraft Book* by Constance Jackson and Judith Plowman, goes against everything we've been told about washing wool, but it really makes handspun wool yarn very soft and fluffy. Wash and rinse the skeins of yarn as usual after spinning. Then fill two containers with water—one with the hottest tap water possible and the other with very cold water. Place the wet skeins in the hot water and allow them to absorb the heat for a few minutes. Then plunge them immediately into the cold water. You'll feel the yarn fluffing in your hands.
—*Roseann Charlton, Coraopolis, PA*

DRYING FLEECE AND WOOLENS

As a spinner and dyer, I spent a long time searching for an inexpensive, simple way to dry fleece and sweaters in my small apartment. I found my solution at a nearby home center in the form of a light-diffusion grid, normally used under fluorescent-lighting fixtures. Not only is the grid inexpensive, but it's also plastic, so it doesn't rust. It's lightweight, and one grid fits perfectly over my bathtub.
—*Debbie Benzer, Ithaca, NY*

THRIFT SHOP YARN

Thrift shops are often a good source for inexpensive knitting and crochet supplies. When I buy yarn that is dusty and musty, I remove the paper band and, without disturbing the hank as it is wound, I dunk it in cool, sudsy water then rinse it. I clip one end of the hank to my clothesline in the breeze out of the sun. When one end is dry I reverse it on the line. If crochet cottons have a spot of dirt on the surface of the ball, I use detergent on the spot, leaving the thread on its cardboard cylinder. If the ball becomes wet, I stuff a paper towel inside the hole, and pin the ball to the clothesline.
—*Helen von Ammon, San Francisco, CA*

KNITTING ABBREVIATIONS

ch	Chain
cn	Cable needle
dc	Double crochet
dec	Decrease
hdc	Half double crochet
inc	Increase
k	Knit
k2tog	Knit two together
LHN	Left-hand needle
lp	Loop
p	Purl
p2tog	Purl two together
p2tog-b	Purl two together in the back loops
psso	Pass slipped stitch over
RHN	Right-hand needle
RS	Right side
sc	Single crochet
sl	Slip
ssk	Slip, slip, knit
st(s)	Stitch(es)
St st	Stockinette stitch
tog	Together
tr	Treble crochet
WS	Wrong side
yo	Yarn over

INDEX

Look for these and other *Threads* books at your local bookstore or sewing retailer.

Beyond the Pattern: Great Sewing Techniques for Clothing

Couture Sewing Techniques

Distinctive Details: Great Embellishment Techniques for Clothing

Easy Guide to Sewing Jackets

Easy Guide to Sewing Skirts

Fit and Fabric

Fitting Solutions

Fitting Your Figure

Great Quilting Techniques

Great Sewn Clothes

Jackets, Coats and Suits

Quilts and Quilting

Sewing Tips & Trade Secrets

Shirtmaking

Stitchery and Needle Lace

Techniques for Casual Clothes

The New Quilt 1

The New Quilt 2

For a catalog of the complete line of *Threads* books and videos, write to The Taunton Press, PO Box 5506, Newtown, CT 06470-5506. Or call (800) 888-8286.